"When I tell my students about peacemakers whose writings on non-violence should be cherished and hopefully put into practice, Gerard Vanderhaar is among them. *Beyond Violence* is still another reason for paying heed to this lasting, moral, and powerful voice."

Colman McCarthy
Director of the Center for Teaching Peace
Washington, DC

"The author offers a fresh look at the nonviolent Jesus, tracing his spirit in all aspects of life: the philosophical, theological, political, and personal. Vanderhaar is a leading authority on nonviolent theory and all his research and lived experience shine in these pages. But it is the personal application of nonviolence that I found most creative. What is the nonviolent stance on abortion? How do you handle your time? How do you deal with a neighbor who is playing a boom box at all hours of the night? What about a mugger? All of these situations are opportunities to live 'in the spirit of the nonviolent Christ.'

"We live in a dark and violent culture. This book is a candle to lead the way into the next millennium."

Mary Lou Kownacki, O.S.B.
Executive Director
Alliance for International Monasticism

"Gerard Vanderhaar presents a vision of the nonviolent Christ that is truly good news. Vanderhaar's compassionate commonwealth is our future, if we are to have one. I recommend this thoughtful, faithful book to all those willing to walk the way of Jesus with such modern disciples as Gandhi, Dorothy Day, and Martin Luther King."

Jim Douglass
Author, *The Nonviolent Coming of God*

"What does active nonviolence mean? Gerard Vanderhaar gives a wonderful map of the realm of peacemaking. He creatively describes both public and private terrain in an engaging style. I was informed and inspired anew to work for peace and justice."

Sidney Callahan, Ph.D.
Author and Psychologist

"This is an eloquent introduction to the life of Christian nonviolence. *Beyond Violence* points us not only beyond the immorality of militarism and greed, but to new life in the Spirit of the nonviolent Christ. Vanderhaar helps us to see with peace eyes. Here is our future—a way to live in Christ's spirit of nonviolence—if we dare accept it."

John Dear, S.J.
Author, *The God of Peace: Toward a Theology of Nonviolence*

"A timely and inspiring book, *Beyond Violence* explores the way of life of the nonviolent Christ—from its biblical foundation to its concrete application in today's world. Whether he's writing about relations between nations or how you spend your money or deal with a difficult neighbor, Jerry Vanderhaar makes the case for Christian nonviolence in a clear and compelling way."

Richard Deats
Editor, *Fellowship*
The Fellowship of Reconciliation

"What we need to do is to operationalize nonviolence, the way an army does its troops, its armaments and ordnance. We need to organize networks and systems of nonviolence, train people by the millions in nonviolence, and, hardest of all, begin living nonviolence. This book shows how."

Walter Wink
Professor of Biblical Interpretation
Auburn Theological Seminary
New York, NY

Beyond Violence

In the Spirit of the Non-Violent Christ

Gerard A. Vanderhaar

TWENTY-THIRD PUBLICATIONS
Mystic, CT 06355

Twenty-Third Publications
185 Willow Street
P.O. Box 180
Mystic, CT 06355
(860) 536-2611
800-321-0411

ISBN 0-89622-739-1
Library of Congress Catalog Card Number 97-60840
Printed in the U.S.A.

Dedication

In memory of the first bishop of Memphis,
Carroll T. Dozier,
a leader with vision and courage.

PREFACE

This book is about nonviolence at the turn of the millennium, about its value for personal spirituality and its guidance for shaping a better world.

For everyone who resonates with the traditions of Christianity, seeing Jesus as the Nonviolent Christ gives a sound spiritual foundation for becoming a more nonviolent person. Living in the spirit of the Nonviolent Christ helps us to move beyond violence in our personal lives, and gives us a clear directional signal for helping our society, our culture, our world move beyond the scourge of violence at the turn of the millennium.

Shortly before he died, Dom Helder Camara, the prophetic archbishop of Recife, Brazil, gave a stirring speech in which he called for "a millennium without misery." The only means to bring about a millennium without misery, given the social trajectory of the world, is through a massive infusion of active nonviolence. Only a widespread, committed, nonviolent spirit, especially in those privileged to be among the "haves" of the world, can create a climate of social justice where all, young and old, healthy and infirm, can have their basic needs met and live in an atmosphere where they can fulfill their human potential. Active nonviolence is in the best interest of all of us.

Twenty centuries ago, Jesus announced the arrival of the Reign of God amid the corruption of religious and political power. Today it is in the best interest of the entire world to follow him and turn around the violence of our day, to confront today's corruption of power that is poisoning our social environment and damning millions to destitution and hopelessness. The Good News for the twenty-first century is that, in and with the Nonviolent Christ, we can successfully confront the culture of violence and make significant progress toward a millennium without misery.

Special thanks to special companions on my nonviolent journey who have provided me with hope and inspiration over the long haul, including: my first Pax Christi Ambassador of Peace colleagues Eileen Egan, Joe Fahey, Bishop Tom Gumbleton, Mary Evelyn Jegen, S.N.D., Dick McSorley, S.J., and Gordon Zahn; in Memphis Rev. Bill Akin, Nancy Abernathy, Julia Allen, Sandy Furrh, Tandy Gilliland, Manuel Soto-Viera, and Deacon Curtiss Talley; formerly of Memphis now in the North Hubert and Lois Van Tol; in Alabama Jim and Shelley Douglass; in California Molly Fumia, Rev. James Lawson, Ginny King, O.P., and Ched Myers; in Connecticut Neil Kluepfel; in Florida Phyllis Turner Jepson and Mary Carter Waren; in Kentucky Chris Dobrowolski, I.H.M.; in Maine Bill Slavick; in Michigan Bill and Mary Carry; in Missouri Jim and Kathy McGinnis; in New Jersey Tonie Malone; in New Orleans Rev. Doug Doussan; in New York Richard Deats and Mike Hovey; in Erie, Pennsylvania Mary Lou Kownacki, O.S.B., and Nancy Small; in Virginia Bishop Walter Sullivan; on the go, John Dear, S.J.; in Europe Bruce Kent and Valerie Flessati, Etienne and Magda De Jonghe; in Israel Abuna Elias Chacour; in the Philippines Fr. Niall O'Brien; my nephews Marc and John-Paul Simon; and for her excellent advice and steady support and loving encouragement over the long haul, my wife Janice.

Memphis, Tennessee
August 5, 1997

CONTENTS

Note to the Reader

Scripture quotes followed by an asterisk (*) are taken from *The Inclusive New Testament*, published by Priests for Equality, Brentwood, MD, 1994. All other Scripture quotes are from *The New American Bible*.

The sources for quotations and research results can be found in notes keyed to the individual text page. This Notes section starts on page 147.

Beyond Violence

PART ONE

The Nonviolent Christ

Jesus was the most active resister known perhaps to history. This was nonviolence par excellence.

—Gandhi

I can do all things through the One who gives me strength.
—Philippians 4:13

ULTIMATE CONCERN

That which we care about the most defines our real faith. That which we value more than anything else defines the direction of our life. Paul Tillich called it our Ultimate Concern. Human beings, he said, are concerned about many things, some of which are quite urgent. Each of them can claim ultimacy for a human life, can command total surrender to its cause. That about which we are in fact ultimately concerned defines our faith, and in doing so makes unconditional demands on us. It also promises ultimate fulfillment.

The much-touted technological revolution has given us twinkling-of-an-eye communication, but it has also enhanced our ability to make war in space. We have access to awesomely sophisticated entertainment. We also face unparalleled spiritual deprivation. Increasing fragmentation and self-centeredness foster a discouragement approaching despair. In our own best interest we seek a guiding light, a solid foundation, an adequate object for our ultimate concern. The Nonviolent Christ and the way of life to which he points provide just such a foundation.

This is not just religion as usual. It is the Jesus of Scripture seen through turn-of-the-millennium eyes as the Nonviolent Christ. And through these eyes we see that the Nonviolent Christ is fully alive, revealing his Presence in new and dynamic ways, showing us how to help in creating a New Heaven and a New Earth through nonviolent love. Active nonviolence is the human spirit's best hope after the twentieth century, the most violent century in human history. Active nonviolence is in the best interest of the peoples of the world in the dawn of a new millennium.

Jesus said that every scribe who has been instructed in the Kingdom of Heaven "is like the head of a household who can bring from the storeroom both the new and the old" (Matthew 13:52*). Nonviolence is one of those storeroom treasures that is both new and old. It's new in the sense that the word itself is a twentieth-century creation, an attempt to put into English the core spirit of Mahatma Gandhi's movement for the liberation and transformation of India. Martin Luther King imported it and made active nonviolence the central feature of his movement for the liberation and transformation of the United States. Gandhi and King showed us that nonviolence is not simply negative, passive, the refusal to respond with violence. It is much more. It is courageous, it is positive, it is using our human powers to change the minds and hearts of those who are perpetrating trouble. It is having the strength to stand up to violence and to provide a humane alternative. Nonviolence, as brought forward by Gandhi and King, is *positive action for true human good, using only means that help and do not harm.* Such deliberate, energized, focused love of a neighbor who for the moment is an enemy can change that enemy's mind and remove the oppression for which the enemy is responsible.

At the same time this kind of nonviolence is old because it always has been the heart of Jesus' life and teaching, even when his life and teaching weren't seen that way. The value of Gandhi and King and other twentieth-century prophets of nonviolence like Dorothy Day and Oscar Romero and Cesar Chavez is in bringing a contemporary freshness to the constant content of the Gospel. They help us focus on the heart of the matter, and perceive it in a way that liberates us to live Jesus' message beyond traditional confines. They show us imaginative ways of dealing with difficult people. They move us past pessimistic resignation to the spreading epidemic of violence. The phrase "The Nonviolent Christ" refers to the living spirit of Jesus, his words and actions seen in light filtered through the prism of twentieth-century nonviolence. The Nonviolent Christ lives in our midst.

CHRIST ALIVE

The historical event of Jesus was, as far as we can tell, modest. He was a village carpenter in Nazareth who heard the fiery preaching of John the Baptist, became convinced that he himself had a special role to play in the coming Reign of God, left his family and profession, and for a short three years traveled the dusty roads of Galilee and the surrounding areas preaching about that Reign. He was what his own Jewish people would have called a Galilean *hasid,* a genuinely holy person, charismatic in his ability to attract followers.

Both his message and his style upset the religious leaders of his day, who turned him in to the Roman occupiers on a charge of sedition. After a cursory examination, the Roman overlord ordered him executed in the torture-death of crucifixion, the brutal fashion the Romans reserved for revolutionaries and runaway slaves. His body was taken down from the cross, wrapped in burial clothes, and deposited in a cave-tomb outside the city of Jerusalem.

End of the Historical Jesus.

Shortly after he was executed, something mysterious happened—something exhilarating, something transforming. Those who had been close to him before he was killed experienced him alive in a new way. They saw him, they didn't see him. They recognized him, they didn't recognize him. He materialized through locked doors then disappeared again. After a short while he was gone altogether. They began to realize that he had not simply come back to life, but much more—he had risen to a new life, a glorified life, a life beyond all death, a life that in some way put a vibrant Spirit into their own lives. Now he was gone physically but, they were convinced, he stayed with them in some transphysical way. They became aware of his spirit, his Holy Spirit, strengthening them, opening their eyes to his true identity. They came to see, in a burst of new-found Pentecost faith, that Jesus of Nazareth was in fact the Messiah, the Christ, the Promised of Ages. He was also, they realized, Son of God in a way no other human person was. Indeed, he was the very self of God living in the world.

They began to spread the word about the Jesus they knew, the Christ, now not only the Jewish Messiah but the Son of God who had the ability to transform lives here and now. They saw him as Jesus Christ, Son of God, Savior. In their enthusiasm they began to take this life-affirming, life-transforming faith throughout Judea and Samaria, then outside Palestine to Syria and Cyprus and Asia Minor and Greece and Rome and eventually to the ends of the Earth.

They first told, then wrote down, what they remembered of his life and his teaching, interpreting him through their new faith vision. They produced the gospels, the epistles, the book of Revelation, that whole collection of writings which was to become our enduring scriptural source of knowledge about him. We can read that treasure of the ages again and again, always in a new light as the circumstances of our life change. When we read it today, we can recognize that this Jesus of Nazareth is the Nonviolent Christ. We see it in the way he acted toward "difficult" people, sometimes gentle, sometimes firm, always truthful. We see it in his sharp rejoinder to those ill-advised religious enthusiasts who would have everyone do it their way. We see it in his prudent and courageous response to those enemies who wanted to kill him. And we see it in his studied assessment of the principalities and powers of his day, the Roman occupation force and its collaborators among his own people. "Give to Caesar what is Caesar's, but give to God what is God's" (Matthew 22:21*), he said, knowing that Caesar has nothing which is not already God's. We wonder why we didn't see Jesus that way before! His nonviolence, our twentieth-century term, is clearly there, but we have to look at the Scriptures in a certain way, through what Richard McSorley calls "peace eyes," to see it.

SEEING

"Have I been with you all this time, Philip, and still you don't know me? Whoever has seen me has seen Abba God" (John 14:9*). "Seeing" is a relationship. We, the ones doing the seeing, gaze upon Jesus, the one who is seen. What we "see" when we look at Jesus has a lot of ourselves in it. It's like when we're thinking of someone we know, then see a stranger and believe for a moment it's the person we were thinking about. Or when we interpret certain facial characteristics as being signs of sorrow or joy or anxiety because that's the way we look when we're sad or joyful or anxious. Any human person we are looking at is subject to nearly infinite interpretations. We bring something of ourself to every "seeing." It's the same thing with seeing Jesus—a combination of what we want and expect to see, and what's really there.

Generations of Christians have "seen" different aspects of Jesus: the divine Son seated at the right hand of the Father; the judge who sends the saved into eternal happiness and the damned into eternal punishment; the sensitive Sacred Heart; Leader of the Crusade; King of Kings; a personal Savior; a spiritual Friend. Seeing Jesus as the Nonviolent Christ is a way of understanding him appropriate to the new millennium. It comes partly from us, from our sense of the importance of active nonviolence in grappling with the culture of violence, and partly from the Jesus of the Scriptures, from his words and actions revealing the way of God.

"No one has ever seen God; it is the Only Begotten, ever at Abba's side, who has revealed God to us" (John 1:18*). God is mystery, incomprehensible. Our human language, our human imagery fail to convey the Awesome Other which is God. All we can say about God, every image we have—Father/Mother, Creator, Judge, Loving, Compassionate, Angry, Just—are projections of human characteristics onto the Mystery. Scholastic theologians called them analogies. Images of God point in a certain direction, but of themselves they are incomplete. They are even misleading, if we take them literally. If we fix on the images too firmly, they become the stuff of which idols are made. The reality of God is beyond all our human images, all our human language. As the Chinese sage Lao Tzu wrote about Ultimate Reality, "Those who say do not know, and those who know do not say." Our language is woefully inadequate to express the Mystery that is God. Those who use that language acting like they know what they're talking about, are in fact unfortunately mistaken.

Happily, though, we have a more reliable way than human language to know God—"Whoever has seen me has seen Abba God" (John 14:9*). Jesus revealed what we can, with better certainty, know about the Mystery. Jesus pointed to himself as the revelation of God. And when we see Jesus as the Nonviolent Christ we know, as John Dear put it, that "our God is Nonviolent."

SPIRITUALITY

Aligning ourselves with the Nonviolent Christ is a safe spiritual bet, because in doing so we position ourselves correctly with our Nonviolent God. Spirituality is often defined as our relationship with God. Put another way, spirituality is our attempt to align our innermost being with the Way of the Cosmos. It is our "attitude," in the sense of the attitude of a space capsule in the proper position for reentry into the atmosphere. Spirituality is our effort to get ourselves right, ultimately right, or at least as right as we can at this time given everything we know. Spirituality is an effort, an attempt, an ongoing discernment. At times it may result in a realignment. When we get a new fix on the Way of the Cosmos, we adjust ourselves accordingly.

We all need a proper spirituality in these anxious times of material abundance for some and spiritual deprivation for many. A proper personal alignment with the nonmaterial realities of the universe is vital. "What people want right now is...the experience that all the religions talk about, the experience of the connection to the divine. They want more spiritual experiences in everyday life, a sense of mystery," as James Redfield put it.

The Psalmist sang, "The heavens declare the glories of God" (Psalm 19:1). Martin Luther King said that the arc of the moral universe is long, but it bends toward justice. The long moral arc of the heavens declares the justice of our Nonviolent God. Since "no one has ever seen God," we can be quite confident that in following the Nonviolent Christ we are aligned with the Way of the Cosmos, in tune with our just and nonviolent God.

A nonviolent spirituality is a way of living out our ultimate concern that is highly appropriate to the tumultuous realities of the new millennium. It has immediate practical consequences. First, it provides a comprehensive philosophy of life, giving us an overview, an interpretation of events, of history, of nature, an insight into what's really happening around us. It shows us how best to get along in our relationships with others, neither giving in nor imposing our will, but seeking what there is of truth and goodness everywhere. It also leads us to see that we need to be nonviolent toward our environment as well.

A spirituality attuned to the Nonviolent Christ constitutes our personal integrity. This is not integrity in the sense of honesty, although it does include honesty and truthfulness, but integrity in the sense of "wholeness." The Nonviolent Christ helps us discern which of our many personal facets to concentrate on, to bring out, to polish, to take on the road to fulfillment—and which to downplay. He helps us acknowledge what is best in ourselves, and also face that which is undesirable—honestly. Humility, Thomas Aquinas said, essentially is acknowledging the truth about ourselves. Aligning ourselves with the Nonviolent Christ is a healthy organizing principle. It helps us become a more integral person. The Nonviolent Christ shows us that a truly human life in our time involves a longing for peace, a hunger and thirst after justice, a willingness to forgive those who have trespassed against us, and a genuine concern for the well-being of our neighbors extending to all of humanity and including especially our enemies. The Nonviolent Christ also shows that such a truly human life will involve suffering for these beliefs as Daniel Berrigan described:

> On the cross we saw One who lived strenuously and profoundly in the Spirit, who with passionate concern to save and succor and heal stretched his arms outward to the world. In Him we saw the human in its suffering apogee. We saw the cost of the human and the glory of God. We saw that the two were one. We saw what we might be.

And we know that we can pursue that vision "through the One who gives me strength," as Paul wrote (Philippians 4:13*).

PRESENCES

Jesus' Great Commission, at the conclusion of Matthew's Gospel, ends with these words: "And behold, I am with you always, until the end of the age" (Matthew 28:20). This powerful promise of spiritual presence holds good today for those who carry on Jesus' mission. Archbishop Oscar Romero insisted, "If they kill me, I will live on in my people." They did kill him. And he does live on. He lives in his people's memory of him in El Salvador and throughout Latin America and beyond. Jesus, too, lives on in memory. But more than memory. "I was hungry and you gave me food, I was thirsty and you gave me drink" (Matthew 25:35). They said we didn't know it was *you*, we only saw someone who was hungry or thirsty. "The truth is, everytime you did this for the least of my sisters and brothers, you did it for me" (Matthew 25:40*). Jesus continues to live in those persons in need who cross our path.

Roman Catholic theology points out other ways in which Jesus is present until the end of the age: in the church, the liturgy, the sacraments; in Scripture; and where believers come together because of him. "Where two or three are gathered together in my name, there am I in the midst of them" (Matthew 18:20). Jesus lives. And we can be confident that the Jesus who lives in the various places where we find him in the gathering of believers, in Scripture, in neighbors in need, is the Nonviolent Christ.

QUESTIONS FOR REFLECTION AND DISCUSSION

1. What are some "ultimate concerns" that people seem to have? How do these concerns affect their lives?

2. How is Christ "seen" by different people you know?

3. Why is it appropriate for our times to see him as the Nonviolent Christ?

4. What do you understand by "spirituality"? How important is it in your life?

5. What personal implications would the Nonviolent Christ have as one's ultimate concern?

Christ furnished the spirit and motivation, and Gandhi furnished the method. —Martin Luther King

GANDHI AND THE GOSPEL

Although it was Gandhi's nonviolent movement that led millions of Christians to appreciate Jesus as the Nonviolent Christ, one must tread lightly in linking Gandhi himself with the Gospel. His roots were firmly grounded in the rich religious tradition of the Hinduism of his native India. Gandhi's first encounter with Christianity was decidedly negative. It occurred when he was a boy growing up in Rajkot, his hometown on India's west coast. This is the way he described it in his autobiography.

> Christian missionaries used to stand in a corner near the high school and hold forth, pouring abuse on Hindus and their gods. I could not endure this. I must have stood there to hear them once only, but that was enough to dissuade me from repeating the experiment. About the same time, I heard of a well known Hindu having been converted to Christianity. It was the talk of the town that, when he was baptized, he had to eat beef and drink liquor, that he also had to change his clothes, and that thenceforth he began to go about in European costume...I also heard that the new convert had already begun abusing the religion of his ancestors, their customs and their country. All these things created in me a dislike for Christianity.

The young Gandhi, with most of his Hindu neighbors, was

disgusted by the Christian practice of eating what appeared to be "burned cattle," and drinking liquor. Some referred to the missionaries as "beef and brandy Christians."

Later, as a law student in England, Gandhi shared his childhood impressions with a new friend.

I met a good Christian from Manchester in a vegetarian boarding house. He talked to me about Christianity. I narrated to him my Rajkot recollections. He was pained to hear them. He said, "I am a vegetarian. I do not drink. Many Christians are meat-eaters and drink, no doubt; but neither meat-eating nor drinking is enjoined by Scripture. Do please read the Bible."

Gandhi took his advice and purchased a Bible. He had difficulty with the Old Testament. The books after Genesis, he said, "invariably sent me to sleep...But the New Testament produced a different impression, especially the Sermon on the Mount which went straight to my heart." Gandhi was discovering the Nonviolent Christ.

Much later, as the undisputed leader of India's independence movement, he did identify himself with Christianity, although not in an exclusive way, but in the context of the humane values that he found in all the major religions. "I am a Christian," he said, "and a Hindu, and a Moslem and a Jew."

Still, he did have special respect for the teachings of Jesus.

If, then, I had to face only the Sermon on the Mount and my own interpretation of it, I should not hesitate to say, "Oh yes, I am a Christian."... But negatively I can tell you that much of what passes as Christianity is a negation of the Sermon on the Mount.

During the long struggle for independence, Gandhi squarely faced his British opponents in the spirit that he found in the Sermon on the Mount. He saw that Jesus' enemy-love means wanting to achieve what is good for the enemy, not giving in to the enemy's demands. It is the basis for Gandhi's three most important principles of nonviolence: *ahimsa, satyagraha,* and the crucial role of suffering. The British responded at first by ignoring him, then ridiculing him, and finally by arresting him. But eventually, because he persevered in a firm, principled love of his adversaries, they negotiated with him until they, too, came to see the wisdom of leaving India as friends rather than continuing to dominate as enemies. What Gandhi had done was to revive and popularize Jesus' Sermon on the Mount in a new cultural context. In doing so he helped generations of Christians to see Jesus as nonviolent and the overall Gospel message as one of nonviolent love. Gandhi showed that the Gospel understood in this light can alter an empire.

AHIMSA

Gandhi insisted that when we are concerned about the genuine good of others, we don't want to hurt them. Hence the emphasis on *ahimsa.* This Sanskrit word, literally "non-harm," expresses the rock-bottom foundation of Gandhi's nonviolence. It means that whatever we do toward others, we try not to hurt them— even when they're doing what we think is wrong, even when they're trying to hurt us. We don't return violence for violence, we don't try to get even, we don't punish. Gandhi may have recalled Paul's advice to leave "getting even" to God. "Vengeance is mine, I will repay, says the Lord" (Romans 12:19). We refuse to return violence for violence out of courage, not out of cowardice, which Gandhi abhorred. He said it was better to be violent than to be cowardly. Where the only choice is between violence and cowardice, he would advocate violence.

> When my eldest son asked me what he should have done, had he been present when I was almost fatally assaulted in 1908, whether he should have run away and seen me killed or whether he should have used his physical force which he could and wanted to use, and defended me, I told him it was his duty to defend me even by using violence.

Ahimsa for Gandhi meant more than refraining from overt harm. It was also internal, it was a frame of mind. It applied even to our thoughts about hurting someone else.

> *Ahimsa* really means that you may not offend anybody, you may not harbor an uncharitable thought even in connection with those who may consider themselves to be your enemy... If we resent a friend's action or the so-called enemy's action, we fall short of this doctrine [of *ahimsa*]. By resenting, I mean wishing that some harm should be done to the enemy... If we harbor even this thought, we depart from this doctrine of *ahimsa*.

In this Gandhi was echoing Jesus' words: "You have heard that our ancestors were told, 'No killing' and, 'Every murderer will be subject to judgment.' But I tell you that everyone who is angry with sister or brother is subject to judgment; anyone who says to sister or brother, 'I spit in your face!' will be subject to the Sanhedrin; and anyone who vilifies them with name-calling will be subject to the fires of Gehenna" (Matthew 5:21-22*).

As muddled humans in a muddled world, we cannot avoid inflicting some harm sometimes. Gandhi said we cannot go through a single day without committing some *himsa*. The important thing, though, in the spirit of the Nonviolent Christ, is to regret it, not accept it easily, certainly not be proud of it.

SATYAGRAHA

Gandhi's second important principle means "the power of truth," truth-force, the search for truth and the strength that comes from relying on the power *(graha)* of truth. Gandhi's intuition of our common humanity led him to the belief that no one has a lock on the truth. All human beings share a common makeup. We all have good and bad points, attributes and failings. We may see part of the truth—quite a bit, even—but those with whom we differ will also have something of the truth. Any one of us may have an angle on it, but so will our opponents. When we step back and look for what may be true and good in their position, we may well come to see things in a new way. When I unilaterally assert the truth I'm convinced I possess, I'm on the road to aggression as I strive to convince others that my way is right, with the consequent loss of whatever truth they may possess. Rather than force them to see it our way and do it our way, Gandhi thought it better to work with them, to be open, to listen, to seek the fuller truth together. He thought we should do this confidently and courageously, secure in the conviction that the truth sought together brings a power that no individual alone possesses.

For Gandhi, *truth was God*. *Satyagraha* implies a never-ending search for truth, which in practice would be a search for God. Gandhi's passion for peace with justice led him to work for what is really good and helpful for everyone. *Satyagraha* means no aggression by me, even in the face of aggression against me. We are all human beings, and we are all struggling. I move forward in the confidence of the truth I possess, but I'm always open to what of the truth the other side possesses. It's another reason not to hurt them.

Truth sought together brings power. Jesus taught that true power comes from working *with* others, not *over* them or *against* them. "You know that those who are recognized as rulers over the Gentiles lord it over them, and their great ones make their authority over them felt. But it shall not be so among you. Rather, whoever wishes to be great among you will be your servant" (Mark 10:42–43). Gandhi taught the same approach. His goal was not just the liberation of India from the British, but a transformation in the British outlook and, indeed, an inner transformation of Indian society. He believed strongly that the attitude of all toward all should be that of service. He said that a person "devoted to service with a clear conscience will day by day grasp the necessity for it in greater measure, and will continually grow richer in faith." Gandhi's faith was the belief in the power of *satyagraha*, and the dismissal of any justification of violence at any level.

The Indispensable Cross
The power of active nonviolence to change minds and hearts,

Gandhi saw, lay in the willingness to suffer—to receive blows rather than inflict them. The nonviolent resister, in absorbing the blows, attempts to show the aggressor that they are both human beings. Violent resistance hardens the aggressor's resolve, and violence escalates. The willingness of the nonviolent person to take blows without fighting back has the ability to reach minds and hearts and cause second thoughts, even change. Gandhi saw it clearly.

> Though I cannot claim to be a Christian in the sectarian sense, the example of Jesus' suffering is a factor in the composition of my undying faith in non-violence which rules all my actions, worldly and temporal.

Taking blows in dignity calls for more courage and self-control than fighting back does. The power of the Nonviolent Christ resides in this willingness to absorb violence rather than give it. Louis Fischer wrote that "The British beat the Indians with batons and rifle butts. The Indians neither cringed nor complained nor retreated. That made England powerless and India invincible."

Inevitably, in confronting a culture of violence with the Nonviolent Christ, we will be faced with those who want to push us out of the way. Most people prefer to rely on violence to get what they want and ward off what is threatening. The Nonviolent Christ calls us to a different decision: to forgo the use of violence. The decision is to say no to it even when we are the object of it. The decision is to substitute receiving violence against ourselves in preference to being violent against others, even in self-defense, even if it means suffering unto death. At that point the decision, with the Nonviolent Christ, is to take up the cross rather than to inflict it on others. As Jim Douglass has said:

> Jesus' vision of life is to take on the suffering of the oppressed not as a passive victim but as one acting in loving, nonviolent resistance, thus risking one's own crucifixion.

The image of Jesus on the cross, the Son of God willing to suffer, is the most poignantly attractive aspect of Christianity. It is indispensable to our understanding of the Nonviolent Christ.

A WAY OUT OF MADNESS

Martin Luther King brought Gandhian nonviolence into American life in the context of the struggle for racial justice. King, as a young Baptist minister steeped in the spirit of the Gospel and thrust into the spotlight of the Montgomery Bus Boycott, was looking for a way to inject Gospel love into the rising tide of racial rebellion. He was unsure how love of God and neighbor could be relevant, apart from individual conduct, to the movement in which he was involved. A new light dawned when he was introduced into the intricacies of the Gandhian campaigns by a Methodist minister, James Lawson, who had served as a missionary in India and came to appreciate Gandhi's depth. King, later describing his personal pilgrimage to nonviolence, said:

> As I delved deeper into the philosophy of Gandhi, my scepticism concerning the power of love gradually diminished, and I came to see for the first time that the Christian doctrine of love, operating through the Gandhian method of nonviolence, is one of the most potent weapons available to an oppressed people in their struggle for freedom.

He found in Gandhi's method the way to make Christian love a practical force for the liberation of his people. He taught them to love rather than hate their oppressors. He led them to express that love in an outpouring of public witness that refrained from personal attacks and always sought dialogue and negotiations. Following Gandhi's example, he was able to identify with the humanity not only of the victims, but also the perpetrators of racial injustice.

Toward the end of the movie *Gandhi*, two of his friends reflect on his life.

"I believe that when we most needed it, he gave the world a way out of its madness."

"He doesn't see it that way."

"Neither does the world."

Gandhi was assassinated in 1948 in the middle of the bloodiest century in human history. The world in Gandhi's time may not have seen that he was offering a way out of murderous madness, but increasing millions of people have come to appreciate it since his death. Gandhi's way leads us to the Nonviolent Christ, who shows us how we can become more nonviolent in our own lives. We can, in a spirit of *ahimsa*, become aware of the many little and not so little hurts we inflict on others during the course of a day. We can, when we're caught up in a feeling of self-righteousness, realize that those with whom we disagree might have some important element of truth, and search for it in an effort to reach the common ground pointed to by Gandhi's *satyagraha*. And, when the chips are down, we too can choose to accept suffering rather than inflict it, recalling the words of the Nonviolent Christ: "You who wish to be my followers must deny your very self, take up your cross—the instrument of your own death—every day, and follow in my steps" (Luke 9:23*).

QUESTIONS FOR REFLECTION AND DISCUSSION

1. In what way can Gandhi be said to have been a "Christian"? In what ways was he not a Christian?

2. How does Gandhi's *ahimsa* differ from cowardice or from passive acceptance of violence?

3. Gandhi believed that everyone can have some aspect of *truth*. Can you see any glimmer of truth in a Hitler, a Stalin, a cult leader like Jim Jones or David Koresh, or a terrorist?

4. Believing that "Taking blows in dignity calls for more courage and self-control than fighting back does" (p. 15) is contrary to conventional wisdom that encourages fighting back when attacked. How could you explain this taking blows to someone who believes in the conventional way?

5. What would it take for Gandhian nonviolence to really be a way out of the madness of violence in contemporary society?

I believe we are on the edge of a quantum leap into a whole new way of organizing and living as a human family.

—Mairead Corrigan Maguire

AN EPIC CHANGE

The end of the Cold War at the beginning of the 1990s was a special moment, one of those great turning points in history. For over half a century the western democracies had had a clear rallying point, a definite enemy. The first enemy was Fascism, from the middle 1930s to the middle 1940s, and the world was plunged into the bloody Second World War during the last decade of Gandhi's life. That horrendous conflict, which killed more than fifty million people, culminated in the nuclear climax of Hiroshima and Nagasaki.

The rubble was still smoking when a new hostility arose, the Cold War between East and West. Scarcely missing a beat, Communism eased into the role of the major enemy of the West. And from the perspective of the socialist countries, Capitalist Imperialism was the foe. The two large surviving military powers, the United States and the Soviet Union, rushed to gain the upper hand in weapons of mass destruction. Gandhi's newly independent India became a pawn in the game for international supremacy, courted by East and West alike.

Both sides saw themselves as right and the other as wrong, in an absolutist and titanic way. Quasi-religious visions developed, preempting the age-old spiritual traditions that held nominal sway. The grounding for the West's vision was the material prosperity of the majority, and the repeated assertion that everyone else could reach that level if they tried hard and the system were allowed to work universally. The grounding point for the East was the *hope* of material prosperity more equitably distributed for all, once the capitalist imperialists were defeated. Their vision was the pot of gold at the end of the Communist rainbow. One young man in China told my wife Janice and me that when he arrived in the United States to attend a university and looked with amazement at the flood of automobiles, prosperous clothes, shelves overflowing with goods of every conceivable kind, his first thought was, "This is true communism!"

Materialism, in the prosperity that already existed for some, or the hope of it for all, became the dominant world philosophy of the Cold War years. But, since human beings cannot live by bread alone, the controlling materialistic philosophy was radically unsatisfactory. Countercultural movements, nourished by the desire for meaning beyond matter, displayed a remarkable resilience. In the East, the quiet persistence of organized religion, especially Orthodox and Catholic Christianity, inward-looking Buddhism, traditional Judaism, and a not-yet-militant Islam continued to attract and hold believers despite determined efforts to suppress them. For many others, belief in unidentified flying objects proved a stubborn kind of faith, despite official repudiations.

In the West, spiritual enthusiasm was sparked by the Second Vatican Council and the ecumenical movement. The vitality of the new state of Israel inspired many. Still others turned to countercultural communes or New Age movements. Many found solace in the individualist spirituality of fundamentalist religion.

The governments of the superpowers remained locked in mutual hostility based on materialistic beliefs and supported by their nuclear arsenals—materialism's demonic manifestation. The fearsome standoff provided a convenient excuse for subduing internal dissent, and for satisfying the power lust by attempting to control neutral peoples around the world. It was taken for granted by most, and expounded explicitly by some, that violence and the threat of violence were absolutely necessary for dealing both with the external mega-enemy, and internal micro-enemies.

Up for Grabs

The end of the Cold War pulled the rug from under this struggle that had been predicated on a clearly defined Enemy. It also brought about a crumbling of the prevailing certainties of progress, self-sacrifice, and expert opinion. No longer was it clear that "our" way was the right way, and that happiness was in everyone's reach. No longer was it taken for granted that sacrifices had to be made for the Cause, because now the long-standing Enemy was melting in a puddle of confusion. Now, on all sides of the Enemy divide, it was everyone for oneself to grab at whatever promised satisfaction at the moment. No longer was it clear, in East and West alike, that expert authority figures had the important answers. They were unmasked as being as uncertain as everyone else about what should be going on, despite their self-assured rhetoric that fooled few anymore. The quasi-religious beliefs of nationalistic, militaristic materialism fell away, leaving a vacuum often filled by quick grasping at whatever political or spiritual movement seemed immediately attractive. Sometimes the vacuum was not filled at all, and despair surged.

Fueled by these uncertainties, the internal dynamic of individual desire began to be increasingly asserted. Although accentuated in the dissolving political realities in the decade of the nineties, the dynamic of desire for individual gratification had always been there, always permeating social and cultural structures. So was the still unquestioned acceptance of violence as a means of satisfying these desires. Given this blind cultural acceptance, it's hardly surprising that, in the absence of the inhibiting restraints of the Cold War, violence should be a widely acceptable means of dealing with problems of getting what one wanted, and of warding off threats to a personal pursuit of happiness.

Violence Yet

At the dawn of the twenty-first century, society seems locked in the grip of violence. Violence is exploited in the media and the entertainment industry. Violence sells. It sells products and it sells fantasies, because of the fascination it evokes. We are simultaneously appalled and attracted by images of violence.

The images abound, and so does the reality. Street crime is spreading, neighborhoods are terrorized. Violence is an epidemic in homes, against spouses, against children. Protection is anxiously sought in guns, legislatures pass laws allowing citizens to carry concealed firearms. The death penalty is increasing in popularity, public opinion clamors for more police, more prisons, and speedier executions. The despair of poverty is driving many to the temporary relief of drugs. Frustration with social currents leads some to blow up government buildings or trade centers or airplanes. Violence on all levels—personal, family, community, nation, and world—penetrates the very fabric of our existence.

The nuclear threat seems long ago and far away, but its shadow is with us still. The five nuclear powers steadfastly resist pressures to eliminate that threat. Existing nuclear weapons, although fewer than at the absurd peak of the 1980s, remain in readiness to wreak incalculable destruction.

There's no question that violence often "works" to secure an immediately desired result. People believe it, and it's true. Criminals can be apprehended and forcibly incarcerated. An intruder can be shot, an attacker disabled. A bully can terrorize little children and take their lunch money. A gunman can rob a bank or a convenience store, can snatch a wallet or purse and get away with it. Military force can put down a riot, or subdue an unruly population. Government-sponsored violence in the form of a strong military with high-tech weapons and the willingness to use them is an international disease. Whether it "works" in the long run, though, is another matter. With the Nonviolent Christ, we believe it doesn't.

Even in the short run violence doesn't work all the time. Someone starts a fight and gets flattened. Most revolutionary uprisings are quelled by military suppression. U.S. violence did not prevail in Korea and Vietnam, nor did Soviet violence in Afghanistan, Russian violence in Chechnya, Iraqi violence against Kurds, the British in India, the French in Algeria, or the police in Los Angeles and New York.

But these failures are easily forgotten. Violence is attractive, seductive. It is propagated by political leaders advocating a strong defense, it's taught in schools as being fundamental to preserve a way of life, and it's headlined by media moguls who have a keen sense of what attracts viewers. No conspiracy exists here. None is necessary. Opinion molders have not gotten together and said we have to spread a climate of violence. They don't have to. Violence is simply the accepted mode of thinking of the vast majority of people, East and West, North and South, who see it as an unquestioned resort for self-preservation. It's so ingrained and so widespread that our times have been aptly termed "a culture of violence."

THE OTHER STORY

But that's not the whole story. Although muted in the media, nonviolence also has been on the rise worldwide in the last four decades of the twentieth century. By the early 1960s both super-powers had sufficient weaponry to wipe each other out as func-tioning societies. The 1962 Cuban Missile Crisis brought the world to that brink. The awesome realization that the violence of war carried to its nuclear extreme could mean the extinction of the human race and the toxic wasting of planet Earth forced millions of thinking people to explore a drastic alternative, a nonviolent alternative. Gandhi's ideas were revisited. In the 1950s the Campaign for Nuclear Disarmament (CND) used Gandhian tactics of public demonstrations in Great Britain to press for the elimination of nuclear weapons. Dorothy Day and other Americans employed Gandhian non-cooperation in refus-ing to take part in air raid drills in New York City.

When Martin Luther King consciously adapted Gandhi's method as the key element in his Civil Rights Movement, he brought nonviolence into the spiritual bloodstream of the West. In subsequent decades, people of all faiths, inspired to look anew into their own religious traditions, achieved impressive results by consciously adapting Gandhi's nonviolence to meet the destructive and exploitative realities of their own societies. Nonviolence was adopted as the central strategy to stop the Vietnam War in the mid-1960s. The Peace People of Northern Ireland explicitly copied King's version of nonviolence in the

1970s. In the 1980s nonviolent protest characterized the campaign against installing tactical nuclear weapons in Europe. Deliberate adoption of nonviolent tactics led to the "people power" uprising in the Philippines which overthrew the dictator Marcos in 1986 without firing a shot. In Latin America, the nonviolent *firmeza permanente,* "relentless persistence," overcame the repressive regime in Chile, gained land for peasants in Brazil, removed the military junta in Argentina, and paved the way for a political transformation in Haiti.

Asia, too, had an outpouring of nonviolence—in China, temporarily interrupted by a military massacre but still alive; in Burma with ongoing protests inspired by Nobel Peace Prize winner Aung San Suu Kyi; softening the harsh government crackdowns in South Korea and Taiwan. The 1996 Nobel Peace Prize spotlighted the nonviolent efforts of Bishop Carlos Ximenes Belo and José Ramos-Hosta to secure the independence of East Timor from its illegal domination by the government of Indonesia.

South Africa, through patient persistence and international pressure, saw the dismantling of apartheid without the widely predicted bloodbath. Country after country in Eastern Europe, through nonviolent citizen action, threw off the Soviet Union's totalitarian yoke to reshape the map of the world. In the explosive Middle East, the tenacious *Intifada* ("to shake off" in Arabic), largely nonviolent although the media focused on rock-throwing young people, eventually moved the Israelis and Palestinians into a peace process. The largely nonviolent uprising in Ciapas in Mexico called the world's attention to the social divisions exacerbated by NAFTA.

The success of the United Farm Workers in securing labor contracts and improved working conditions for the long-exploited and largely Latino agricultural workers was due to their nonviolent tactics. Nonviolent demonstrations in East and West held the nuclear threat in check. They also prevented the invasion of Nicaragua, which was seriously planned in the 1980s. Prayerful, nonviolent vigils beside the railroad tracks, as the White Train passed through the countryside of middle America carrying its deadly load of nuclear warheads, literally stopped the train from running. The Department of Energy decided to substitute inconspicuous eighteen-wheelers for the highly visible train that was arousing the curiosity of people as it rolled through their neighborhoods. Richard Deats summarized what was happening:

> While "nonviolence is as old as the hills," as Gandhi said, it is our century in which the philosophy and practice of nonviolence have grasped the human imagination and exploded in amazing and unexpected ways, as individuals, groups, and movements have developed creative, life-affirming ways to resolve conflict, overcome oppression, establish justice, protect the earth, and build democracy.

While the twentieth was an unprecedented century of violence, it was also an unprecedented century of nonviolence, giving all who follow the Nonviolent Christ solid empirical grounds for adopting nonviolence as our own personal life-style, the expression of our own personal spirituality.

With the hope engendered by the Nonviolent Christ we anticipate, as Mairead Corrigan Maguire did, a major move, a quantum leap toward a nonviolent outlook, toward a new, nonviolent way of living as a human family.

QUESTIONS FOR REFLECTION AND DISCUSSION

1. Can you see a connection between desire for self-gratification and the spread of violence? How would you describe the connection?

2. Why does violence sell?

3. What does it sell?

4. If *nonviolence* really is widespread now (pp.22-24), why don't we hear more about it in the mainstream media?

5. Where do you see nonviolence in your immediate circle of experience?

It is absolutely inappropriate for anyone to feel psychologically comfortable in this day and age. —Helen Caldicott

THE CHALLENGING SELF

In our more pessimistic moments, the dream of living a non-violent life can seem impossible to fulfill. It's like we're trapped by a psychological AIDS, powerless to turn the tide, doomed to be crushed by our surrounding culture of violence. Whatever we do is not enough. Indifference and cruelty seem to be the order of the day.

Paul gave us an apt image for the fray: "Our struggle is not with flesh and blood but with the principalities and powers, with the world rulers of this present darkness, with the evil spirits in the heavens" (Ephesians 6:12). At times it appears that this culture of violence is beyond flesh and blood, that its source is awesomely and powerfully trans-human. A friend of ours calls it "The Devourer," invoking a biblical image: "Your opponent the devil is prowling around like a roaring lion looking for someone to devour" (1 Peter 5:8).

Let's stop and get a fix on these principalities and powers, this Devourer, these evil spirits that seem to be frustrating our efforts to follow the Nonviolent Christ. Who are they? Where are they?

SATAN'S TRICKS

André Gide said, "Satan's greatest trick is to convince us he does not exist." That was a wise warning in the face of the naive optimism of his time, the early decades of the twentieth century. More recently, toward the end of the same century, René Girard observed, "Satan's second greatest trick is to convince us he does exist." Whatever its source, and it's ultimately inexplicable, something tremendously Evil has been loosed in this century of world conflagrations, genocides, and nuclear terrorism. We do well never to underestimate the reality of Evil. It's strong, it's pervasive. We neglect it at our peril.

Tempting as it is to put the blame elsewhere, we do know that a great deal of responsibility exists much closer to home. The biblical drama in the Garden of Eden presents an image of Evil, teaching that we and every other human being in the history of the human race are born with a tendency toward it. We need to face this reality of the human condition, and not blame Evil entirely on an outside diabolic force. Holding on to a Source of Evil outside ourselves allows us to shift the blame, to shrug in despair, and to put the whole thing off as a cosmic struggle in which we're only the pawns. Richard Woods put it this way:

> Today, few believe in a personal devil, although the mystery of evil still haunts the consciences of us all. And we are no doubt as prone as were our ancestors to focus our fears and concretize them, ever anxious for a scapegoat who will once again prove to us our own guiltlessness....Our contemporary attempts to reify the source of the myriad disasters and tragedies of life, producing "evil spirits" behind every bush and new ideology, are, as they always were, an escape from confronting the challenges of historical existence with all the attendant risks of failure through personal weakness, ignorance, and malice. The demonic is ourselves.

The reality is that all of us have the capacity to hurt, just as all of us have the capacity to help. A fundamental truth about ourselves is that we are a mixed collection of good and bad components. In Israel Charny's words, "Human beings are at one and the same time generous creative creatures and deadly genociders." We have the power to create, and the power to destroy. The world we live in contains, as Charny put it, "both a glorious epic of achievements and love and a dreadful blood-soaked nightmare of destruction." The problem of Evil is rooted in ourselves. We have the capacity to take part in the glorious achievements and also in the blood-soaked destruction. We feel the attraction of our noble yearnings. We are also attracted by the lure of our lower leanings.

As violence is rooted in our capacity for evil, nonviolence, too, has to begin with oneself. It doesn't end there, certainly, but it does start there. Anyone who would follow the Nonviolent Christ accepts the imperative of being more nonviolent *within* oneself and more nonviolent *toward* oneself.

NOT QUITE THERE

Unfortunately, the self is notoriously slippery. We can never say, "There, it's done. I'm a nonviolent person. Now I'll go out and spread the spirit of the Nonviolent Christ." The self presents a constant challenge. It will continue to be a challenge until we check out of this life altogether. Gandhi as an old man was asked how he was faring in the struggle against his own anger. "Not very well, I'm afraid," he said. "That's why I have so much sympathy with the other scoundrels in this world."

Ancient Christian wisdom, dating at least from Gregory the Great in the seventh century, identified seven Capital Sins, called "capital" because they give rise to other personal problems. The seven were pride, covetousness, lust, anger, gluttony, envy, and sloth. These seven dangerous tendencies are part and parcel of the human condition. They are dangerous because, if unchecked, they impel us into actions which are harmful to ourselves and to others.

At the same time, these tendencies provide opportunities for nonviolent expression.

Pride, stemming from the natural inclination to think well of ourselves, can lead to inordinate self-esteem, seriously overestimating our abilities and our good qualities. It can upset our relationships, push us to grab for the limelight, to step over—or on—others to reach a pinnacle we think we rightly deserve but we don't. It leads to a drive for power, an effort to bend others to our will, one of the identifying evils of our age.

Nonviolence within ourselves, in the spirit of Gandhian *satya-*

graha, would have us steadily searching for the truth about ourselves, recognizing both the gifts with which we have been graced
and the limitations that are part of our particular makeup.
Nonviolence toward ourselves would have us celebrate our gifts
and accomplishments in a true spirit of humility which is a hum-
ble spirit of truth, of telling it—and listening to it—as it really is.

Covetousness is the desire for possessions, for material
goods, particularly those we see others having and we don't. In
our competitive culture, covetousness is constantly stimulated;
first, by the pressures of advertising to turn us into ever more
voracious consumers with the assumption that wealth is good
and more wealth is better, and second, by the media halo around
a life-style of luxury, which fosters the greed that is another
identifying evil of our times.

Gandhi expressed the nonviolent approach: "If each retained
possession only of what was needed, no one would be in want,
and all would live in contentment." The key is to discern what
we really need. Nonviolence toward ourselves does not mean
denying those genuine needs. It means trying to fulfill them
while keeping them from escalating into mere wants.

Lust is another media-fanned flame in western society. Part of
the flame is a reaction to the stifling of legitimate sexual expression that has plagued puritanical societies everywhere. But other
flickers in the flame are callously introduced to stimulate con-
sumerism.

Nonviolent sexuality encourages us to enjoy the goodness
inherent in the desire for union. It also respects the dignity of
the persons with whom one would unite so that no exploitation
or harassment occurs. We try to keep our sexual desires within
socially acceptable bounds, and at the same time we look carefully at those socially acceptable bounds to make sure they are
in fact nurturing rather than damaging.

Anger, too, lurks in us as an ever-threatening outburst in the
face of frustration. At times we will, beyond our control, feel
angry, upset, wanting to lash out at what is harassing us. Like
Gandhi, we recognize our ability to become angry, and know
that we can hurt others when we let our anger loose.

Becoming more nonviolent within ourselves entails a constant effort to curtail the lashing out. It does not mean curtailing the tendency to anger itself. There are times when we should feel angry, times of righteous wrath, times when we need anger's energy to stop the tanks in their tracks. Being nonviolent within ourselves means recognizing the anger, and channeling it so that it doesn't break out and hurt anyone.

Gluttony, like lust, is a by-product of our innate desire for pleasure. It too is subject to the pressures of overabundant production and the incessant drive to sell the food and drink that are produced. These economic pressures have spawned the phenomenon of "grazing," going around with a can of drink or a package of chips perpetually in hand, eating absently while we go about our business.

Nonviolence would have us regulate our food intake, not suppress it. We are encouraged to eat and drink with delight. Dorothy Day liked the simple Catholic Worker fare, but wanted it prepared with care. "We had baked potatoes for supper, and cabbage overspiced. I'm in favor of becoming a vegetarian only if the vegetables are cooked right!"

Envy is a feeling of resentment because someone else possesses an advantage that we would like to have ourselves. It can lead to verbal putdowns, even physical violence.

The honesty that comes with *satyagraha* counters envy by encouraging us to appreciate not only what we ourselves already have, but to respect and even rejoice in the qualities and achievements of others. Because envy is corrosive and preoccupying, Gandhi's *ahimsa* leads us away from doing this psychological damage to ourselves.

Sloth, laziness, is another function of our physicality. We want to be comfortable, we want to feel good, we like to take it easy. Giving in too much can lead to dereliction of duty, or doing the minimum just to get by. It's easy to be seduced by comfort.

On the other hand, some giving in is necessary for our health. We need, in Jack Armstrong's training rules of half a century ago, "plenty of fresh air, sleep and exercise." Or, as a cartoon character expressed it, "At my age, Happy Hour means time for my nap." A nonviolent person would set appropriate goals for oneself, factor in the importance of taking care of physical and mental capacities, then act to fulfill those goals no matter how uncomfortable it might sometimes be.

Get On with It

Because the slippery self never seems to be in quite the condition we want it to be, we can succumb to another seduction—an endless preoccupation with self-improvement. It's possible to become so obsessed with one's imperfections, so desirous of shaping up this or that aspect of our personality or appearance, that we never commit ourselves to the real work of creating the Kingdom of God. Constant fretting about wanting to be better is contrary to the Nonviolent Christ, who would have us get on with the mission. Paul threw himself into the mission despite whatever imperfection constituted his "thorn in the flesh" (2 Corinthians 12:7). And although the daily cross Jesus asked us to take up primarily means the opposition encountered from opponents of the Nonviolent Christ, it sometimes refers to those personal imperfections of which we're painfully aware. But after a decent go at them, we decide we've got to get moving after the real prize.

During the season, an athletic team mixes practice with performance. It's never a matter of refusing to play the game until we get it perfect in practice. The team practices, the team plays, the team practices again. Following the Nonviolent Christ means getting out there to work for a just peace while keeping an alert eye on the recalcitrant self. Just as practice helps a team improve its game performance, the experience in the game makes the team better. So with ourselves. Being aware of the possibilities of greater nonviolence within ourselves makes us more effective in acting nonviolently toward others. And our experience with active nonviolence toward others makes us a more nonviolent person within ourselves.

Psychological Discomfort

As long as we're on this side of the grave we'll never be a finished product. There's no getting there and then living happily ever afterward. In the meantime, there's plenty of work to be done. That's why Helen Caldicott could say that it's inappropriate to feel psychologically comfortable in this day and age—in any day and age. That's why Edward Schillebeeckx could say that the Peace of Christ consists in an "inward discontent," because the situation in the world and within ourselves is not as it should be. I often hear people say that the world's problems are too big. They just can't get involved. The Nonviolent Christ says yes, they are big, but you can get involved anyway. You can get involved by becoming informed of what's happening, paying attention to the news. You can get involved by communicating with people who share your values, who also want to do something, however modest, to help. And then we can all take part in at least some of these efforts.

With the Nonviolent Christ we accept the challenge—to become more nonviolent within ourselves and toward ourselves, and to help create a more compassionate and more nonviolent world outside of ourselves.

QUESTIONS FOR REFLECTION AND DISCUSSION

1. Are there any aspects of violence in our world that really do seem to have their source outside the human condition?

2. If everyone is weakened by sin, can anyone be truly nonviolent? What is the best we can hope for?

3. Besides the seven Capital Sins described in this chapter, name several other human vices that are commonly encountered in today's world. How can each of these also provide an opportunity for *nonviolent* expression?

4. Since we can never reach perfection in this life, we always have to be aware of our shortcomings. How can we balance this awareness with the need to take part in socially constructive activities, that is, why shouldn't we devote most of our energies to self-improvement?

5. What is your answer to the statement that the world's problems are too big for us to get involved?

CHAPTER FIVE

You can no more win a war than you can win an earthquake.

—Jeannette Rankin

No Good Violence

It's about time we came to the recognition that *there's no such thing as morally good violence.* Our culture was founded in revolutionary violence, is sustained by utilitarian violence, and has a monopoly on apocalyptic violence, yet the conviction is spreading that none of this violence is morally good, none of it can be justified in good faith, with a right conscience.

Although rooted in Jesus' life and teaching, this conviction is ahead of the curve of mainstream Christian tradition that has held sway for the past seventeen centuries. That tradition, embodied in the Just War Theory, held that violence under certain conditions can be morally right. In practice this tradition enabled Christians to support any war in which their country was engaged. It also at one time supported the torture and killing of religious dissidents, and has consistently upheld, but with diminishing enthusiasm, the right of states to put to death citizens guilty of serious crimes.

Let's be clear. When we speak of violence we mean *the exertion of physical or emotional force to injure or abuse someone.* We're not talking about damaging or destroying *things.* We're referring strictly to violence that hurts *people.* Violence is often physical, but it can also be emotional, as in intimidating someone without laying a hand on them. Violence can also be structural, when people are hurt by being unable to break out or rise above harmful societal influences. "Poverty is the worst form of violence," Gandhi said.

The common assumption (so common that it's rarely questioned) is that when someone does it to me, that's "bad" violence. But when I defend myself and strike back, that's "good" violence. When an enemy starts an unprovoked war, that's "bad" violence. But when our side musters the troops and rallies our resources to stop them, that's "good" violence. Theological and ethical tradition has been more refined, factoring in motivation, end and means, double effects. But its bottom line has been that while most violence is bad, some can be morally good, even virtuous. The Nonviolent Christ has helped us cut through this ethical fog.

The belief that good violence is sometimes necessary to counteract bad violence is what Walter Wink has called the Myth of Redemptive Violence. It's deeply ingrained in popular culture. Most people unquestioningly affirm that sometimes violence is necessary to correct matters that have gone astray, and that such violence is "good."

The foundation for the Myth of Redemptive Violence is what Joseph Campbell called the War Myth. This is a view of the human environment as a jungle. If we're not constantly on our guard, others will take advantage of us. It's a depressing way of looking at things, to consider life, in Thomas Hobbes' words, as "solitary, poor, nasty, brutish, and short." But it's a common way. And to many, depressing as it is, it's realistic. They see it as the way things are, and consider those who believe differently to be at best naive, at worst foolish and dangerous. As one U.S. senator expressed it, "Even in a world where the lion and the lamb are about to lie down together, we Republicans are committed to the principle that the United States of America must always be the lion."

VIOLENCE VEILED
Some violence might seem pragmatically useful. A temporary goal can be achieved by beating someone over the head, shooting to stop an intruder, or conquering another country. But the Nonviolent Christ leads us to see that the means used to achieve these purposes are contrary to the dignity and decency that is

the inalienable right of every human being. No one forfeits that right. All violence hurts—the victims, primarily, but also, in some deeper sense, the perpetrators.

Committing an act of violence, deliberately harming another person, has a corrosive effect on the personality of the perpetrator. A former police officer testified, "I'll tell you something. It's hard to kill a man. If you have to use deadly force, it's going to change your life. And it's not going to be for the better." Daniel Berrigan observed that in any violation of the dignity of other human beings, even in a revolution that overthrows an unjust regime or a war that repels an unjust aggressor, one's moral character is diminished. "There is a cruel lesson here... Concentration on the sight of a gun inevitably contracts the bore of the mind." Mao Zedung, famous for his adage "Power comes from the barrel of a gun," was himself personally diminished and corrupted after the triumph of his revolution when he settled in to absolute power in the palace of former emperors in the Forbidden City in Beijing.

Inflicting hurt violates fundamental human dignity. This is a hard truth. It goes against the social grain. "Our" violence, which because it's ours must therefore be "good," is marked by flags, veiled in patriotic oratory, blessed by religious officials, upheld by courts, praised by parents, and hailed by historians. Words like "force," or "use of the military instrument" or "collateral damage" have masked the violence of war. "National security" is the myth covering the clandestine violence committed by intelligence agencies. "Protecting our vital interests" is the rationale for armed intervention anywhere in the world. "Seeing justice done" is the euphemism for the premeditated killing that is capital punishment. "Taking up arms against a repressive regime" is another word for revolutionary violence. Military personnel on one side who kill large numbers on the other side are decorated for "heroic bravery." The torture of religious dissidents is presented as "defense of the faith." The torture of political dissidents is called an unfortunate necessity to preserve public order and the stability of the regime.

But it's ugly all the same. As Voltaire said, "Killing is murder, except when done to the sound of trumpets." Underneath the flags and behind the orations is the reality of people deliberately inflicting severe damage and even death on others.

Gil Bailie said that when violence is unveiled, it is revealed for what it really is: *violence,* doing harm to other human beings, violating their personal dignity.

> There have been periods of history in which episodes of terrible violence occurred but for which the word violence was never used...Violence is shrouded in justifying myths that lend it moral legitimacy, and these myths for the most part kept people from recognizing the violence for what it was. The people who burned witches at the stake never for one moment thought of their act as violence; rather they thought of it as an act of divinely mandated righteousness. The same can be said of most of the violence we humans have ever committed.

UNMASKING IT

The Nonviolent Christ removes the veil of justifications that have traditionally covered the violence of "just" wars, self-defensive homicide, executing criminals, disciplinary cruelty against children. The Nonviolent Christ shows us that, no matter what we call it, we're dealing with an affront to human dignity.

And it's downhill from there. Once inflicting death and suffering is accepted as a method of achieving a goal, Daniel Berrigan observed, "people become strictly unnecessary except insofar as their lives are slightly more useful than their deaths." Human beings become expendable, for the sake of whatever Cause—winning the war, overthrowing the tyrant, restoring domestic tranquility.

The Nonviolent Christ helps us reject this whole Myth of Redemptive Violence with all its works and pomps and misrepresentations. The Nonviolent Christ shows us a better way, takes us down another path, illuminated by the conviction that there is *always* a more decent, more humane, and usually more effective way of dealing with these matters than by violence. The

Nonviolent Christ undermines all the rationales used to justify violence. Gil Bailie put it this way:

> As the New Testament writers somehow amazingly understood, the cross destroyed the delusions on which conventional culture had always depended, namely, the delusions that make it possible for a culture to vent its violence on a scapegoat without feeling any moral pangs for having done so. By "raising up" before the world the victim of such scapegoating, and by showing that the powers that killed him and the worldly and religious authorities who tried to lend moral legitimacy to this murder were deluded—"they know not what they do"—the cross began the slow but irreversible process of destroying the myths of sacred violence.

Human beings are not beasts of prey; life need not be solitary, poor, brutish, and short. All of us are made "in the image and likeness of God" (Genesis 1:16). Weakened by sin, yes, but freed from its slavery by Jesus "in whom we have redemption, the forgiveness of sins" (Colossians 1:14). The Nonviolent Christ helps us believe in the innate decency of everyone, even in those whose conduct is at the moment despicable from our point of view. Despicable conduct might be emotionally upsetting, even enraging, but it offers no excuse for violence against its perpetrators. Gandhi said we might as well do violence to ourselves:

> It is quite proper to resist and attack a system, but to resist and attack its author is tantamount to resisting and attacking oneself. For we are all tarred with the same brush, and are children of one and the same Creator, and as such the divine powers within us are infinite. To slight a single human being is to slight those divine powers, and thus to harm not only that being but with him the whole world.

REGRET IT
Violence there may be, *himsa* we may commit. But we do a great disservice to truth when we gild that violence in fool's gold,

when we pretend that it's right and just and *moral.*

But we learn this from the Nonviolent Christ, we don't learn it from our culture. The Nonviolent Christ places us fundamentally at odds with a culture of violence. Daniel Berrigan wrote:

> In a fallen world, we will probably always have some forms of violence. But the question is, what part can Christians play in such a situation? To say that the world is fallen and sinful is not to say all that needs to be said. We still have the Sermon on the Mount and the example of Jesus Christ.

From the Sermon on the Mount and the example of Jesus we learn living love, active compassion. The Nonviolent Christ teaches that "There is no greater love than to lay down one's life for one's friends" (John 15:13*). To be prepared to *die* for one's friends, yes, but not to be prepared to kill. If we are provoked, and if we do succumb, the appropriate response is to regret it, be sorry, repent, acknowledge our failing. As Gil Bailie said:

> Jesus' ethic is clear: to suffer violence rather than inflict it. As Christians, we are called to imitate him. We will fail, but when we do, let's not return home from our failure to ticker-tape parades. Let's fall on our knees and pray for God's forgiveness. If the question is: Is there any violence for which I would not need to repent after having committed it? The answer is no.

From the Nonviolent Christ we learn to face the truth about ourselves, to regret our violence, not pretend it's laudable. From the Nonviolent Christ we also learn courage in the face of danger. We do *not* learn weakness, timidity, sitting back and letting them beat on us, turning away while others suffer. The Nonviolent Christ would have us intervene, but as nonviolently as possible. We intervene out of love, first for the victim, but also out of love for the perpetrator.

THE CONTINUUM

We might think of a sequence or progression of values with "pacifism" or complete nonviolence at one end, and what Duane Cady has called "warism" or "good" violence at the other. True pacifism, in light of Gandhi and the Gospel, is a commitment to resolve conflicts through *nonviolent* means. Warism, at the other end of the continuum, is the belief that force can be the most effective way of solving a problem, that violence can compel an enemy to submit to our will, whether on the personal, social, or international level, and that sometimes we have no choice but to use that force.

Pacifism and Warism are emotionally charged words. To accuse someone of being a warist, a warmonger, is to evoke a caricature of a heavily armed fighter, believing in the law of the jungle, a steely-eyed zealot for might makes right. Warism's calmer proponents advocate that, while violence should always be undertaken reluctantly, there are times when it is justified in defense of persons or property or national sovereignty.

Frequently, too, pacifism is conveyed in a caricature as an absolutist conviction that it is always wrong to use force against anyone, no matter who is going to get hurt. The caricature is the basis for discussions that begin, "So you're a pacifist. What would you do if your grandmother was about to be raped?" Joan Baez says she would answer the question this way:

"I'd yell, 'Three cheers for Grandma!' and leave the room."
"No, seriously. Say he had a gun, and he was about to shoot her. Would you shoot him first?"
"Do I have a gun?"
"Yes."
"No. I'm a pacifist, I don't have a gun."
"Well, say you do."
"All right. Am I a good shot?"
"Yes."
"I'd shoot the gun out of his hand."
"No, then you're not a good shot."
"I'd be afraid to shoot. Might kill Grandma."

What Joan Baez was doing was dismissing the caricature in favor of a more accurate picture of what pacifism really is. It is not appeasement, not giving in or selling out. It is an attitude of refusing either to meet violence with violence or to bow down in the face of it. It is an attitude of engagement, of respect for opponents and enemies, of searching for peaceful means of resolving conflicts.

The Nonviolent Christ points us in the direction of the pacifist end of the spectrum. This, we believe, is the way Jesus would have us live—without, however, judging or looking down on those who have different and sincerely held convictions, and without simplifying the complexities of common security or crime prevention or incurable suffering. Reaching out to others beyond ourselves, being concerned for their genuine good, is the energy that emanates from the Nonviolent Christ. In the spirit of the Nonviolent Christ, we accept others where they are, not where we would like them to be. Respectful dialogue, in the interest of searching for more complete truth, is considerably more productive than arguing for the purity of a position.

The Nonviolent Christ gives us a more balanced view of human nature than that presented in the Myth of Redemptive Violence. Human nature is not fundamentally aggressive and in conflict, although it possesses the ability to be so and at times actually is. The world need not necessarily be a threatening, competitive, hostile environment, although it possesses the ability to be so and at times actually is. Much more often, however, it is a place of opportunity for growth. Human nature is more cooperative than competitive. The Nonviolent Christ teaches us, as did Jeannette Rankin, that no war can really be won any more than an earthquake can be won, that no violence can be good violence. We're convinced that people, no matter how difficult things may be, can go beyond differences and live together in a sufficient degree of harmony. Once we put aside the distinction between good violence and bad violence and opt instead for nonviolence, we enter a new era in our life. When the spirit of the Nonviolent Christ breaks into consciousness, it is a counter-cultural experience with unsettling—but exhilarating—consequences. We feel like we're waking up to the dawning of a new day. Everything looks different. Whatever lies ahead we don't know. But we're going to meet it in a different way.

QUESTIONS FOR REFLECTION AND DISCUSSION

1. What are instances of violence that are seen as "good" by some and "bad" by others?

2. Name several contemporary "veils" that cover violence in our world.

3. Describe several stages on the continuum between "warism" and "pacifism."

4. Do you personally know any people who would fit the description of a "warist"? Do you know of any public figures in this category?

5. How would you answer the accusation that refusing to use violence at times is an evasion of responsibility, for example, in protecting one's family from someone who would injure them?

Mounting an expedition to actualize a Compassionate Commonwealth of all peoples...is the great spiritual challenge of our time.   —Sam Keen

THE CITY OF GOD REVISITED

The Nonviolent Christ would guide us in building the City of God. This image comes from St. Augustine's classic work of political theology, *De Civitate Dei*. Augustine (354-430) was bishop of Hippo in what is now Algeria in North Africa. He wanted to give a coherent analysis of the confusing politics of the Roman Empire and the Christian Church. The part of his book that pertains to our nonviolent concern described the City of God as one of two coexisting societies. The other is the *Civitas Terrena,* City of This World. These two societies exist side by side, intermingled.

The first, Augustine said, was a city of the spirit, the other a city of the flesh. He used "flesh" in the same sense as St. Paul: "Now the works of the flesh are obvious: immorality, ...hatreds,...acts of selfishness,...dissensions...and the like" (Galatians 5:19–21). "Flesh" means that which drags us down, our tendency to sin. "Spirit" is that which lifts us up, the nobility in our character. "Spirit" in the City of God is not the ethereal as opposed to the corporeal, as though the body were bad. It means the best, most decent tendencies of the unified human person, flesh and blood, mind and heart.

"Two societies have issued from two kinds of love," Augustine wrote. The love of God in Christ produces the City of God. The love of self to the exclusion of God produces the City of This World. The City of This World is characterized by war and dissension, by violence and the lust for domination. In the City of God, on the other hand, "all citizens serve one another in charity."

When we follow the Nonviolent Christ, we serve one another in charity. Jesus had said that he "did not come to be served but to serve" (Matthew 20:28). Huston Smith, describing the spirit of Hinduism, said that the beginning of religion occurs when people advance from the goals of pleasure and success and turn outward to help others. The Letter of James defined religion, pure and undefiled, as: "coming to the aid of widows and orphans when they are in need, and keeping oneself uncontaminated by this world" (James 1:27*). In turning the vector of our energy outward from helping ourselves exclusively to helping others as well, we act as John the Baptist did when he said, pointing to the Messiah, "He must increase; I must decrease" (John 3:30). We may decrease physically in the expenditure of energy or decrease financially in the depletion of resources, but spiritually we increase beyond measure.

The service that builds the City of God takes many shapes and forms, continually interacting with the currents of contemporary culture. Sometimes it's direct help, as in visiting the sick, sheltering the homeless, teaching the inquiring, nourishing their spirit. Sometimes it's indirect, as in advocacy for public policies that heal rather than hurt, or changing social systems from exploitation to liberation. In the powerful parable of the sheep and the goats in Matthew 25, Jesus makes service of those in need the sole criterion for a favorable Judgment. Those who helped "the least of my sisters and brothers" will "inherit the kingdom prepared for you from the creation of the world" (Matthew 25:34*). Those who don't "will go off to eternal punishment" (Matthew 25:46*).

A venerable Baptist minister once said, "There's not a job in the world that's not ninety percent janitoring." Cleaning, painting, and fixing is part of our service. Martin Luther King advised young people who were confined to less attractive jobs to "sweep streets like Michelangelo painted pictures." My wife Janice and I saw people sweeping streets like that throughout the cities of China. Sweeping streets with dignity is service. Advocacy for legislation to provide housing for the homeless is service. Pushing banks to provide home improvement loans in low-income areas is service.

Augustine's City of God gives us an urban image for what we know from Scriptures as the Kingdom of Heaven. Matthew, in deference to the sensitivity to the Divine Name in his predominantly Jewish Christian readers, almost always used "Heaven" for what the other gospels call the Kingdom of God. The Kingdom has a definite this-worldly component. Those who would be specially blessed in this Kingdom would be the poor in spirit, those who mourn, the meek, those who hunger and thirst for justice, the merciful, the pure in heart, the peacemakers, as Jesus characterized them in the Sermon on the Mount (Matthew 5:3–10). Those also would be specially blessed who show us the way to a healing relationship with the earth. Those who would receive the most attention and the most concern would be the blind, the lame, the sick, the deaf, the handicapped, prisoners, anyone in need of healing and liberation.

COMPASSIONATE COMMONWEALTH

"Kingdom" is another of those words that has become problematic today. The image of King connotes patriarchical and absolutist rule. In the world of biblical times, a world of authoritarian kingdoms and powerful patriarchical kings, the image of God's Kingdom was subversive. It meant someone other than the present earthly ruler was in charge. Rosemary Ruether pointed out that

We are led to a recognition of Jesus as the iconoclastic prophet who chastised the existing social and religious hierarchies for lording their power over those subject to them. In doing this...Jesus sought to reverse the [existing]

social order, making empowerment and the liberation of the oppressed the meaning of servanthood....Jesus tried to teach that right relationship with God rejects a dominant-subordinate model in which the relationship between God and human beings is used to justify any type of oppression.

We grope today to find an appropriate phrase that conveys the ideal relationship among human beings beyond anything currently existing, a phrase that is both subversive and constructive. I like Sam Keen's image of Compassionate Commonwealth. It's a transnational, transcultural, global symbol for the Kingdom of Heaven, the City of God, especially apt as we move into the dawn of the twenty-first century.

The Compassionate Commonwealth as Keen described it is a world characterized by positive peace and social justice. But it is not here yet. We are in the time of becoming, of seeing the direction and attempting to walk in it. More than that, we're helping bring it about. To do so we have to turn away from acceptance of nationalism and sovereignty as a basic principle, moving in the direction of an effective world federation of government. We put an end to a belief in never-ending material prosperity in favor of sustainable growth. The Compassionate Commonwealth means a complete rejection of a world divided between rich and poor in favor of a more just distribution of wealth. In the Compassionate Commonwealth we use resources in a way that is in harmony with the total environment. We do not look at nature solely as the supplier of raw materials and recreational facilities. We recapture respect for the natural world as an integral part of creation of which we humans are also an integral, but not dominant, part.

By whatever name—City of God, Kingdom of Heaven, Compassionate Commonwealth—we look to the culmination of goodness in earthly affairs—in human affairs, yes, but more than that. Human beings are the consciousness and conscience of all earthly creation. We're coming to appreciate our role not as lord and master but as a component of the whole.

The Compassionate Commonwealth has already begun with Jesus. "The reign of God doesn't come in a visible way. You can't say, 'See, here it is!' or 'There it is!' No—look: the reign of God is already in your midst" (Luke 17:20–21*). Begun with Jesus, we help it along with the Nonviolent Christ, who has given us a glimpse of the plans.

GUIDING LIGHTS

The Nonviolent Christ, through his model of resistance, helps us develop skills essential for organizing the Compassionate Commonwealth. In the Sermon on the Mount, Jesus offered a realistic guide to how to act in the face of adversity, when our reflex of self-preservation comes into play. It's a guide that preserves the humanity and dignity of both sides in a conflict, and an essential guide for developing the Compassionate Commonwealth. "You have heard that it was said, 'An eye for an eye and a tooth for a tooth.' But I say to you, offer no resistance to one who is evil" (Matthew 5:38). In the context, this means offer no *violent* resistance. But don't just give in, don't just sit back and take it. Rather, offer *nonviolent* resistance. Passivity in the face of aggression validates the effectiveness of the aggression, shows that it works.

So does fighting back in kind. Fighting back justifies further violence by the aggressor. Jesus taught to offer definite opposition, but make the opposition nonviolent. He explained what he meant with several examples. "When someone strikes you on the right cheek, turn and offer the other" (Matthew 5:39*). The *right* cheek is the key. It signals that the blow was an insult, an emotional injury more than a physical one. In that case, Jesus taught, show the insulter you know what's happening. Stand in quiet dignity, effectively saying, "All right, you've insulted me. I'm not going to insult you back or defend myself. If you want to insult me again, go ahead." This might well cause the insulter to take a second look at what's happening, and provides the person an opportunity to stop. It's resistance, but it's nonviolent resistance.

"If anyone wants to sue you for your shirt, hand over your

coat as well" (Matthew 5:40*). In Jesus' time, going to law over
a shirt would only happen to a poor person unable to repay a
debt. Okay, if you want to take the clothes off my back, take
everything, including my coat. I'll go naked. Again, the idea is to
jolt the creditor into recognition of what is being done to this
poor person.

Similarly, "Should anyone press you into service for one mile,
go two miles" (Matthew 5:41*). Jesus' listeners would have recognized here a practice common to the occupying Roman sol-
diers. They were allowed by their military regulations to force
civilians to carry their heavy packs, but for no more than a mile.
Then they had to cajole someone else into carrying the pack a
second mile. By voluntarily offering to carry the burden another
mile, the person would put the soldier in a dilemma. If he
accepted the offer, he would be disobeying regulations. If he
rejected it, he would have to look around for someone else to
press into service. The soldier might, in the moment of confusion, come to realize the burden he and his comrades were
putting on the people of Palestine, not just in forcing them to
carry the packs, but in the whole oppression of military occupation.

So Jesus' alternative to violence was not passivity, it was nonviolent *resistance*. Throughout Jesus' life and teaching, the message is clear. Don't sit back and take it, but *do something* in the
face of unwarranted aggression. It's what Jesus himself did when
on trial before Caiaphas and again before Pilate. He didn't simply accept the accusations silently, he spoke back to both officials in a way that commanded respect.

Earlier he had said, "But to you who hear I say, love your enemies, do good to those who hate you, bless those who curse you,
pray for those who mistreat you" (Luke 6:27–28). Turning the
other cheek, praying for those who mistreat us, are prototypical
expressions of the Nonviolent Christ. When someone attacks,
absorb the blows initially. Don't fight back and escalate the conflict. Approach the attackers with genuine concern. At least bless
them and pray for them. And then reach out to them. Meet them
with positive, calculated, constructive action. Turn the other

cheek in quiet dignity. Offer to go naked, or to carry the soldier's burden a second mile. "If your enemies are hungry, feed them; if they are thirsty, give them drink. For in doing so, you will heap burning coals on their heads" (Romans 12:20*).

The Nonviolent Christ provides us with the architectural design for the City of God, the Compassionate Commonwealth: positive action for true human good, using only means that help and do not harm; courageously standing up to opposing forces; being willing to take blows rather than give them; knowing that some goodness resides in everyone no matter how unpleasantly they may be acting at the moment; overcoming our fears and anger to reach that goodness, confident in the power of redemption over retribution and revenge.

WHEAT AND WEEDS

Augustine saw how we live in the City of God and the City of This World at the same time. The characteristics of both Cities are all around us. Two loves continue to produce two Cities. At any moment we can tilt more toward one than toward the other. In the dawn of the twenty-first century we struggle to build a more peaceful world in the midst of a culture of violence, a milieu of self-interest and anxiety that often erupts in violent actions, causing terrible damage. This is the milieu in which we attempt to live our nonviolent spirituality—because this is also a milieu of expanding nonviolent awareness. Jesus gave us an image of the mixture:

> The Kingdom of Heaven is like a farmer who sowed good seed in a field. While everyone was asleep, an enemy came and sowed weeds among the wheat and then made off. When the crop began to mature and yield grain, the weeds became evident as well. The farmer's workers came and asked, "Did you not sow good seed in your field? Where are the weeds coming from?" The farmer replied, "I see an enemy's hand in this." They in turn asked, "Do you want us to go out and pull them up?" "No," replied the farmer, "if you pull up the weeds you might take the wheat along

with them. Let them grow together until the harvest, then at harvest time I will order the harvesters first to collect the weeds and bundle them up to burn, then to gather the wheat into my barn." (Matthew 13:24–30*).

At any moment we, and others leaning in the same direction, live side by side with those leaning the other way, toward the culture of violence. We're not talking about good and bad people here, but about all of us who, at any time, will be tilting more toward the City of God, or toward the City of This World, toward those growing the wheat of service, or those growing the weeds of self-centeredness.

The Nonviolent Christ has given us a revolutionary tactic for transforming a violent world into a Compassionate Commonwealth. We have a searchlight to help us locate humane values in murky political messes. The Nonviolent Christ gives us a fine, steady confidence for finding our way through the maze of our culture of violence that is in our own best interest, and the interest of all humanity. It is, as Sam Keen said, *the* great spiritual challenge of the new millennium.

Questions for Reflection and Discussion

1. St. Augustine said that in the City of God "all citizens serve one another in charity." Where do you see such service happening in your world?

2. In what kinds of service are you personally engaged?

3. Which image do you prefer for a society of service: City of God, Kingdom of Heaven, or Compassionate Commonwealth? Why?

4. The *Civitas Terrena,* the City of This World, Augustine wrote, "is characterized by war and dissension, by violence and the lust for domination." Where do you see neighborhoods of the City of This World?

5. When confronted by the City of This World, the Nonviolent Christ would have us turn the other cheek, hand over our coat, go a second mile. What would be the hoped-for outcome of such responses? Is such hope realistic?

PART TWO

PERSONAL NONVIOLENCE

It belongs to the very substance of nonviolence never to destroy or damage another person's feeling of self worth, even an opponent's. We all need, constantly, an advance of trust and affirmation.   —Bernard Häring

The first essential characteristic of nonviolent action is that it is creative. —Hildegarde Goss-Mayr

CLOSING DOORS SOFTLY

Thomas Merton once said that when he undertook to become nonviolent, he started by closing doors softly. Personal nonviolence is about this kind of sensitivity. Although the Nonviolent Christ points us to the whole world, the litmus test of a nonviolent spirit is closer to home. It's how we get along with those immediately around us. Our global nonviolence is hollow if we are hurtful to our family, our neighbors, our colleagues, those whom Dietrich Bonhoeffer called "the nearest Thou at hand."

The foundation of personal nonviolence toward all of these is Gandhi's *ahimsa*, the determination not to harm, not even to be thoughtless or careless. Lao Tzu wrote, "One may move so well that a footprint never shows, speak so well that the tongue never slips." He was advocating ways of bringing about the ideal harmony that exists when people are careful and considerate. Being sensitive to others, trying to avoid offending even in little things, is a way of becoming more nonviolent to the nearest Thou at hand. With those who are upset by unpleasant, obtrusive noise, a nonviolent person not only closes doors softly, but is careful to keep other sound makers subdued, like a television set, heavy footsteps when neighbors live underneath. Active people in motion in an enclosed area can bump into one another when both are absorbed in their tasks. Janice and I know that when we're preparing supper together we have to do what we call the dance of the kitchen—keep moving, but avoid collisions.

COMMUNICATION

As we express ourselves in normal conversation, ordinary interchange, we have ways of saying things that can be more agreeable or less agreeable. *Ahimsa* leads us to choose an alternative expression when the first one that comes to mind is abrasive. Words that imply fault can be irritating, like "Oh no, you certainly made a mistake there," or "You shouldn't have done that." Nonviolent speech changes such remarks to a positive observation. "Well, so that's what happened." Few people appreciate unsolicited advice about what they "should" do or "should not" have done. It implies that one's conduct leaves something to be desired. When somebody tells me, "You should not have said that or gone there or acted that way," I begin to feel defensive. When I even say to myself that I should have done something differently, I feel a twinge of guilt. A counselor friend calls remarks like these "shouldies." They are usually not helpful, can be positively irritating, and are almost always futile.

We did what we did, and maybe we made a mistake. If we did we're sorry, but we don't need to wallow in what might have been. It's important to learn from the past, to see where we went wrong, and figure out how we might act differently if similar circumstances arise, but it's not helpful to get bogged down in a quicksand of guilt and regret. If we don't like it when others push us into that quicksand, we try to avoid doing it to them. No more "shouldies."

Using gender-inclusive language is another nonviolent skill akin to closing doors softly. Language has not yet fully adapted to the rapidly spreading awareness of gender equity. Some are very alert to this and notice quickly when the older, now inappropriate, language forms are used. A nonviolent person will be sensitive to antique language. For "mankind" we substitute "people" or "human beings" or "humankind." Rather than "man a project" we can "staff" it, or "use personnel" or "get people to do it." To speak of a "woman doctor" or "male nurse" prolongs stereotypes of professions formerly associated with one gender or the other. They are now simply doctors or nurses. We may hasten to add a sentence with a "she" or "he" if we sense a misunderstanding. "Fire fighters," "mail carriers," "police officers" are preferred terms to replace the "men" previously identified with these occupations.

Besides the actual words we use, nonviolent speech will also incorporate certain humanly enhancing conversational techniques. We will, for example, speak to others as equals when we're in a position of authority, unless that would make the other person uncomfortable. Conversely, when we sense that someone prefers to be addressed by a formal title like "Mr." or "Mrs." or "Doctor" or "Father" or "Reverend," we will call them that. The spirit of *ahimsa* leads us to use the term of address that makes the other most comfortable.

We will also be careful to share the floor and not monopolize conversations, and especially not to interrupt when others are speaking. If it pleases some people to think that when they talk, people listen, a nonviolent person will be content with "When I listen, people talk."

In the spirit of nonviolence we are careful to follow up on promises made. When we easily say we will do something, then fail to deliver, we may leave someone in the lurch, or disappoint those who were anticipating our accomplishing what we said we would do. Better to be cautious about undertaking commitments than to agree quickly but find that we are unable to fulfill, or that we forgot.

Because we are verbal creatures and speech is natural, it's easy to say things we don't mean, blurt out thoughtless remarks, or even use our words deliberately to deceive. Although we may get away with it in our words, it's much harder to regulate the physical expression of what's on our mind. That's why body language is the most reliable mode of communication. Even when we don't understand someone else's language, we can communicate through a smile, through expressive gestures and bodily movement. During a two-hour taxi drive from Quito up into the mountains of Ecuador, I fumbled and strained to speak with the driver in the little Spanish I knew. Janice didn't even try Spanish. She used smiles, gestures, and animated English, and had a wonderful exchange with him even though they didn't understand each other's words.

Sometimes a discrepancy arises between what people say with their words and what they do with their eyes, their face, their hands, their posture. Or the discord may be between what they proclaim and the way they live. A wise person said, "What you are speaks so loudly, I can't hear what you're saying." We do well to place our trust more in what we see than in what we hear.

Others observe us in the same way. To project confidence when standing, we can keep arms loosely at our side, not folded across our chest indicating self-protection—and certainly not clasped together in front in the fig-leaf position, which communicates awkwardness, hesitancy, and creates a feeling of unease. We can be careful about eye contact, too—always some, but never too much. We look people in the eye when we speak to them, both individuals and groups. It enhances their trust. But four or five seconds at a time is enough for one individual. More than that and we seem to be staring, which is discomfiting. Look, look elsewhere, then look back.

Also discomfiting is invading others' personal space. Americans feel most comfortable, except in moments of intimacy, with three or four feet of distance between themselves and others. Getting closer can seem like an invasion. It stirs a vague response of suspicion, a little anxiety.

As we try to live more nonviolently, we take care that our own body language is as nonabrasive as our spoken language. A calm, quiet, poised demeanor, a relaxed, upright posture, give reassurance to those who observe us. A nonviolent person would want to be different from the upset man Mary Lou Kownacki described: whenever he entered a room, people immediately began rearranging the furniture. In the spirit of *satyagraha* we strive to make our nonverbals harmonious with what we are saying, and both truthful to our inner convictions.

Albert Camus observed that after thirty we begin to be responsible for our own face. He was getting at the connection between our inner state of being and the outward look we display to others. Some feel that no one should care how they look because it's inner integrity that counts, not outward appearance or grooming or clothes. A few good friends will always feel comfortable no matter how we look. Others may not. Attempting to be pleasant in relatively minor matters like appearance will ease the atmosphere and spread a sense of comfort to those around us.

PUBLIC RELATIONS

Ellen Goodman wrote about a friend who has taken what she called a vow of civility.

> Starting now, she will not only ratchet up the pleases, thank yous and would-you-minds, but also the friendly eye contact and the small daily conversations that are so trivially labeled as "mere pleasantries." They do not seem so mere to her anymore. She has resolved to liberally apply the lubricant of pleasant social exchanges to her brittle urban village.

Civility is one expression of closing doors softly in a hectic, harried world. It's one step everyone can take to counteract the culture of violence. It won't change the big picture, but it will create an aura of personal peace. It is a sign that we care for the people with whom we come in contact. As Goodman says, "in the end, 'manners' are about treating others as if they matter."

Our public relations, our interactions with those we encounter in public, includes nonviolent driving. We drive nonviolently when we yield to allow another car to enter the traffic flow, when we refuse to retaliate when cut off, when we use the horn sparingly if at all, when we refuse to take offense at a crude gesture made in our direction.

Our public civility conveys a positive recognition of those who serve us in stores, restaurants, gas stations, supermarkets. So often these attendants are treated like machines, useful for computing what a customer owes, taking the money, giving back the change. In our nonviolent public relations we treat them as persons appreciative of acknowledgment, not as robots.

Smiling is a nonviolent gesture understood in every culture. Except at times of grave seriousness when a smile is inappropriate, we are well advised to have a smile at the ready at all times. One peacemaker advised, "Smile at children—of all ages. Even if they are about to throw a rock at your car, they will often be disarmed by a wave and a smile." When someone is angry with us on the phone, try a smile. They won't see it, but our voice will convey pleasantness, and the anger often subsides.

Merton's soft door closing and Goodman's civility are apt metaphors for *ahimsa* toward every Thou at hand in our public relations.

TO EAT OR NOT TO EAT—WHAT

The Nonviolent Christ reinforces in us a respect for *all* life— human especially, but also animals and plants. The spirit of the Nonviolent Christ makes us sensitive to every living creature, and uneasy about the taking of any life. The Nonviolent Christ encourages respect for our natural environment, protecting it, using only what we have to for our own support, refusing to hunt or fish for sport, hesitant about capturing and taming animals, forcing them out of their natural habitats and incarcerating them in the artificial atmosphere of zoos. While we may not go as far as some Jains and refuse to kill a mosquito or wear a gauze face-covering lest we inadvertently injure a gnat, we do show an appropriate respect for every living creature, animal and vegetable.

Many peace people are vegetarians. They don't want to be involved in killing animals, and they don't want to be eating animals others have killed. They know that a meatless diet is healthier and contributes to a higher energy level. Conscious of the nonviolent use of money, they know that a meatless diet is more economical. It also puts them in solidarity with the majority of people in the world who can't afford to eat meat, ever.

Gandhi was a vegetarian, but he refused to insist that others follow him in this.

Meat-eating is a sin for me. Yet, for another person, who has always lived on meat and never seen anything wrong in it, to give it up simply in order to copy me will be a sin.

Gandhi also thought it necessary to kill animals who were threatening the community's food supply. For him, the dignity and decency of human beings took precedence over other forms of life.

> If I wish to be an agriculturist and stay in the jungle, I will have to use the minimum unavoidable violence in order to protect my fields. I will have to kill monkeys, birds and insects which eat up my crops. If I do not wish to do so myself, I will have to engage someone to do it for me. There is not much difference between the two. To allow crops to be eaten up by animals in the name of *ahimsa* while there is a famine in the land is certainly a sin.

Some taking of life, though, is necessary for human support. We do need to eat. But, in the spirit of the Nonviolent Christ, it should be done respectfully. Lin Yutang put it this way: "If a chicken has been killed, and it is not cooked properly, that chicken has died in vain." Native Americans asked forgiveness of the animals they killed for food, out of reverence and respect. Jesus apparently was not a vegetarian. He multiplied fishes as well as loaves, partook of the Passover seder which included lamb, and, when a guest in someone's home, ate whatever was put before him.

Life also extends beyond animals into the whole world of plants. Eating vegetables also involves destroying a form of life. A realistic assessment of the food chain includes the recognition that eating necessarily involves killing something. Alan Watts' insight is helpful in coming to terms with the destructive side of eating. Watts advised cultivating an attitude of respect and gratitude for those creatures whose life has been taken that we might eat.

> The very least I can do for a creature that has died for me is to honor it, not with an empty ritual, but by cooking it to perfection and relishing it to the full. Any animal that becomes me should enjoy itself as me....Every form of life killed for food must be husbanded and cherished.

In building the City of God, we need a comprehensive environmental impact study. We want the Compassionate Commonwealth to preserve and harmonize with, not destroy, our natural surroundings. What we eat and how we eat it should be harmonious with our whole personal nonviolent outlook. Although we never finish coping with our ever-challenging individual idiosyncrasies, our personal nonviolence will simultaneously be attuned to the vibrancy of all life that surrounds us.

QUESTIONS FOR REFLECTION AND DISCUSSION

1. Thinking about your life _at home,_ what actions could you take that are comparable to Thomas Merton's closing doors softly?

2. After reading the section on "Communication," have you noticed times in your own conversations where _nonviolent_ words or communication modes could have been used? Examples?

3. Thinking about your life _outside your home,_ what opportunities present themselves for civility, for closing doors softly?

4. What is your personal feeling about eating meat? How, in a spirit of nonviolence, can you talk about it with people who disagree with you?

5. In view of the pressures from the City of This World, the weeds growing in the midst of the wheat, how much energy should you spend on the equivalent of closing doors softly?

CHAPTER EIGHT

It is a penance to work, to give oneself to others, to endure the pinpricks of community living. —Dorothy Day

"DIFFICULT" PEOPLE

Gandhi's personal secretary Mahadev Desai once penned, after a particularly frustrating encounter with the Mahatma:

> To live with the saints in heaven
> Is filled with bliss and glory.
> But to live with a saint on earth,
> Well, that's a different story.

Anyone who upsets us, causes us grief or anxiety, is at that moment being difficult. If it's a momentary encounter, we can be polite, say goodbye, and walk away. We don't have to have a lasting relationship with the difficult person. But if it's someone we need to live with or work with or associate with over a longer time, then we can't just be polite, say goodbye, and walk away. Well, we can, and sometimes prudence dictates that we should, but it doesn't solve the problem. The difficult person is staying around, and continues to be difficult. Our attempts to withdraw leave a residue of frustration that will accumulate a pile of poison that corrodes our sense of well-being and pushes us perhaps toward an angry outburst. The Nonviolent Christ reminds us that we need to love our neighbors when they're being difficult—especially when they're being difficult. Dorothy Day called it a penance to endure the pinpricks of living with people who sometimes proved difficult.

JESUS' DIFFICULT PEOPLE

A number of people became troublesome for Jesus. From the moment he went public, Jesus experienced misunderstandings with Nazareth neighbors and even with his family. Shortly after his baptism by John and the revelatory experience about his own mission, Jesus went back to his hometown. During a Sabbath synagogue service when he implied that he was fulfilling a messianic prophecy, people who had known him from childhood were so incensed at his seeming delusion of grandeur that they hurried him out of town and tried to throw him off a cliff! Jesus slipped away, but his subsequent visits to Nazareth were few and far between. He chose not to stay and engage the hostility of his scandalized neighbors. His hour of supreme sacrifice had not yet come.

Instead, he established his base of operations in Capernaum, near the Sea of Galilee. Reports on his astonishing activities there filtered back to his family. "When his relatives heard of this they set out to seize him, for they said, 'He is out of his mind'" (Mark 3:21). They traveled to Capernaum to get him and bring him back home, for his own good—and, presumably, theirs as well. No family's reputation is helped by having a son that almost everybody in town thinks is crazy. Mark's Gospel describes what happened when his mother and brothers arrived in Capernaum.

> Standing outside they sent word to him and called him. A crowd seated around him told him, "Your mother and your brothers and your sisters are outside asking for you." But he said to them in reply, "Who are my mother and my brothers?" And looking around at those seated in the circle he said, "Here are my mother and my brothers. For whoever does the will of God is my brother and sister and mother." (Mark 3:31–35)

He refused to go back with them, refused to submit to their anxious care. To have played into their misperceptions would have been contrary to the truth of who he was and what he was about. His refusal was a way of showing love for them, tough love, perhaps, but genuine love in light of the bigger picture.

The broader implication of the story, the reason it stuck with the early church, was their conviction that the community of believers engenders ties that are similar to those in a family. The story is an antidote to tribalism at any level, including the family. The bonds we share with others "who do the will of God" are as strong as family ties—spiritually, if not emotionally. They transcend gender, race, ethnic identity, national allegiance. Treat every one of the community as we would treat our brothers and sisters.

We know from the rest of Jesus' family story that his mother stood by him to the end. And early Christian tradition identified two of his chosen Twelve, Jude and the lesser James, as his brothers. Whether they actually were we don't know for sure, but at least part of the family followed and supported him.

Contemporary tribalism reared its head when a recalcitrant Samaritan village refused to offer hospitality to Jesus and his band because they were on their way to Jerusalem. Samaritans thought Jerusalem a highly improper place of worship, and considered those who did worship there to be outside the pale. Most Jews, reciprocally, thought Samaritans were dead wrong with God. James and John, the Sons of Thunder, were indignant at the slight shown them by these inhospitable Samaritans. They wanted to retaliate, swiftly and conclusively. "Lord, do you want us to call down fire from heaven to consume them?" Jesus rejected this divine napalm strike, saying, in effect, "Look, fellows, we don't do things that way." "Jesus turned and rebuked them, and they journeyed to another village" (Luke 9:51–56). The message to all later generations of Christians was to swallow an insult given out of a misperception. If we're secure in what we're about, we don't have to battle back every time someone offends us.

Peter also was the victim of a misperception. He absolutely could not comprehend Jesus' prediction of his coming suffering. "'God forbid, Lord! No such thing shall ever happen to you.' [Jesus] turned and said to Peter, 'Get behind me, Satan! You are an obstacle to me. You are thinking not as God does, but as human beings do'" (Matthew 16:22–23). Jesus' abrupt reaction must have hurt Peter. But they had been through a lot together, and Jesus was confident of Peter's rock-like loyalty. Although Peter was taken aback by the vehement putdown, he gamely stuck it out, and eventually did understand what the Nonviolent Christ was all about.

Sometimes Jesus simply removed himself from the presence of difficult people. Once it was to escape from religious zealots who were pestering him.

Pharisees came forward and began to argue with him, seeking from him a sign from heaven to test him. He sighed from the depth of his spirit and said, "Why does this generation seek a sign? Amen, I say to you, no sign will be given to this generation." And he left them, got into the boat again, and went off to the other shore. (Mark 8:11–13)

At other times he just had to get away from everybody, difficult or not, to find a little breathing room, quiet time to nurture his spirit in prayer and reflection. As his fame increased and people sought him out at all hours, he had to take time out.

The report about him spread all the more, and great crowds assembled to listen to him and to be cured of their ailments, but he would withdraw to deserted places to pray. (Luke 5:15–16)

Jesus displayed a variety of reactions when people proved difficult. Sometimes he did not stay and engage, as with the Nazareth neighbors or the Samaritan villagers or the pestering Pharisees. He was "keeping his eyes on the prize," and knew he had to get about his messianic mission. With others, like his immediate family or Peter, he felt he could jolt them into acknowledging that he really wasn't crazy or misreading the signs, that they had to stretch to understand his involvement in bringing about the Kingdom of Heaven. For all of us who reflect on these stories down through the ages, he's the Nonviolent Christ, nudging us into trying to love those difficult people who keep turning up in our lives as they did in his.

HOW ON EARTH TO LOVE THEM

It wouldn't be so hard if only they'd change, if they would stop doing whatever it is that makes them difficult! We may fervently wish for such a change, and may even try to push it in the assurance that we're right and these others really ought to do things our way. The Nonviolent Christ encourages us to explore more deeply, to ponder three questions: What is there about this person that is creating the difficulty? Second, what is there about me that makes him or her difficult? Then, in light of the answers to the first two, what can I do to make things better between us, that is, how can I realistically love this difficult person?

We start by making a list of the problematic person's annoying traits. Maybe it's being too pushy, too critical, too insensitive, too demanding. Maybe it's being too volatile, too emotional, too unreasonable. Or maybe it's in another direction, like being too shifty, too uncooperative, untrustworthy. It could just be that the person has taken a puzzling dislike to me.

In drawing up the list of annoying traits, we have to be careful of stereotyping. We need to stay focused on the individual, not on a group of which he or she is a part. Stereotyping is attributing to all in a certain category the unpleasant characteristics that may exist in a few. "Police are violent." "Marines are brutal." "Gays are promiscuous." "Feminists advocate abortion." "Arabs are devious." "Rich people are insensitive." We need to make sure we don't find this particular Marine difficult because we assume that all Marines are brutal and we don't like brutal people.

An especially difficult individual for me personally is one who seems to have all the answers, and wants others to do it his or her way. I resonate with Sam Keen who says, "Obedience is a virtue for children and a civic obligation, but not a good way to spiritual maturity." I am leery of anybody who claims to have *the* answer, who has discovered *the* secret of life, who has the *best* therapy for what ails us. Such a person rubs me the wrong way.

We needn't shy away from the annoyance list on the pretext of avoiding uncharitable thoughts. *Satyagraha* calls us to search for the truth, no matter how unpleasant, as a constant process of figuring out how to get along, as an essential element of active nonviolence. Otherwise we're into denial. The list of flaws we've drawn up is the truth, as we see it. Here it is, firmly fixed in my mind or even on paper.

The second question is not quite as comfortable. What is there about *me* that makes this pushy person unpleasant, this volatile individual unsettling, this elusive one frustrating? Maybe we cling a bit too much to stability, we're not flexible, we can't roll with being bossed around, told what to do. We want to be in control. We want this pushy person to get out of our face, leave us alone. The volatile, emotional individual disturbs our sense of order. We like predictability, and become uneasy when someone changes directions quickly. Emotional outbursts make us uncomfortable. We prefer to be quiet. Obtrusive displays of emotion disturb us. The elusive one is difficult because we value reliability, steadiness, and have a hard time adjusting to someone whose behavior seems to keep changing.

Okay. We've got a list about what's wrong with the others, and we've started to identify some of our own characteristics that make us sensitive to these difficulties. We press forward. Are some of their traits actually characteristics about ourselves that we don't want to face? A common psychological mechanism is to project onto others an unpleasant characteristic we ourselves possess and then dislike them because of it. We often do this when we are unable to come to terms with something in ourselves that we subconsciously consider a weakness—my annoyance at the know-it-all, for example. In my honest moments, I'm aware that I'm also one of those who feel I have quite a few answers, or at least the important ones, and I don't like it when someone else claims to have answers different from mine.

It's also possible that deep down I really want to dominate others, to have them do things my way. But I don't admit it to myself, because I don't like to think of myself that way. So when I look at this difficult person with a whole array of good qualities that I ignore but focus instead on the person's pushiness or bossiness, demanding conformity, I am irked precisely because it's something I don't want to face in myself. Being righteously peeved at the other is a way of compensating for my own inner control drive.

Or I may be afraid of my emotions, have a hard time letting go. I'm what others call uptight, but I don't like to admit it. So I react negatively to lively, outgoing, vivacious people, wishing they'd calm down. Perhaps the one I dislike for being shifty and uncooperative is really being reserved. But because I don't reveal myself easily and keep my own defenses up, I project an unpalatable evasiveness on the other. And about those who simply don't like me, well, I may harbor doubts about my own self-worth, but I don't like to acknowledge that I have a level of insecurity. So when others seem to disapprove of me or reject me, rather than seeing it as the normal give and take of human relations, I see it as a flaw in them. Some people just don't like the way others are. It's no big deal. *De gustibus non est disputandum.* There's no disputing individual tastes.

EASING THE DIFFICULTY

"Test everything; retain what is good," as Paul advised (1 Thessalonians 5:21). The first big therapeutic step in dealing with the difficult people in my life is to look as deeply and as honestly as possible into myself and see if, by chance, any of the disturbing qualities in the difficult person have roots in my own psyche. If the answer is yes, then the direction for making things better is clear. I've got to get about changing myself, or at least acknowledging and accepting what I have previously denied. I have to face the fact that I like to be right, to have answers, to see people looking to me for guidance. So I have to be especially careful of making absolute truth claims myself. There's a big difference between proposing ideas and insisting that others accept them. I have to be careful I don't become "difficult" for others in this way.

But if the answer is no, the problem is not very much in me at all, then I go back to looking at the difficult person. What is there about her or him that may be behind the unlikeable behavior? Psychology tells us never to underestimate the pervasive power of fear in human motivation. Fear can lead to flight, causing people who are excessively fearful to become timid and withdrawn. But fear can also lead to striking out. People who are dominating, pushy, demanding, may well be constructing a defensive facade to prevent others from hurting them. They fear the emotional blows and subconsciously intuit that the best defense is a good offense. Come on strongly to others and they will be reeling backwards and won't be able to hurt me. Personal inadequacy is almost always behind efforts to hurt others emotionally or physically. Aggressors are attempting to counter their own feelings of inner pain. They are able to make some headway with it when they see others become inadequate or suffer pain, too. One way to insure that is to create the pain for them.

So when I see people who are difficult because they are demanding, or because they are sarcastic, or even because they are cruel, I do well to suppose initially that their behavior is motivated by fear. Behind their mask is a weaker, more fearing ego struggling to survive in the midst of threatening hazards. Knowing that this is probably what's happening gives me a good sense of direction in attempting to love these particular difficult people in the spirit of the Nonviolent Christ.

QUESTIONS FOR REFLECTION AND DISCUSSION

1. Do you know anyone who has a good reputation outside but who, like Gandhi, is sometimes difficult to live with inside?

2. What do you think of the accounts of Jesus' reactions to the difficult people in his life?

3. Can you identify any "difficult people" in your own life? Concentrate on three or four. What is it about each of them that makes them difficult?

4. Still concentrating on those same three or four difficult people, what is the source of the difficulty, *why* are they this way?

5. Is there anything you can, with integrity, change within yourself to ease the difficulty?

God grant me the courage to change the things I can, the patience to accept the things I can't, and the wisdom to know the difference.

—The Serenity Prayer

NEGOTIATION NOW

D orothy Day once observed that sometimes it seems better to have "a good, thorough, frank outgoing war, rather than the sneak attacks, stabs in the back, detracting, defaming, hand-to-hand jockeying for position that goes on in offices and 'good works' of all kinds." She was well aware of the many difficult people she encountered in going about her life. She herself reached out creatively to those who found refuge in her Catholic Worker community. Her creative love for difficult people gives us a vibrant model of nonviolence. When people live together or work closely together, conflicts are bound to arise. Rather than evade them, it's better to engage them nonviolently. As psychiatrist Arthur Kornhaber put it, "You may have a fight, but if you're committed to each other, you come out the other end."

Martin Luther King said, "I plan to stand by nonviolence, because I have found it to be a philosophy of life that regulates not only my dealings in the struggle for racial justice, but also my dealings with people, and with my own self." His tragic assassination deprived him of the opportunity of spelling out how the philosophy of nonviolence regulated his dealings with other people. But in the decades since his death others have expanded the implications of nonviolence in interpersonal interactions.

We now have many ways of adjusting the techniques of Gandhian nonviolence for dealing with the difficult people we encounter in our own life. They don't dilute what Dorothy Day called the penance of the experience, but they often lead to surprisingly amicable outcomes.

If one were to give a name to the day-to-day tactics of getting along with difficult people, it would be *negotiating*. Nonviolence on a practical level of dealing with people with whom we have differences is always a matter of negotiating. Negotiation is a patient effort, involving communication on various levels, in an attempt to work through our differences and come to some mutually satisfactory working relationship. The outcome may not be permanent. As long as difficult people remain difficult, we will have to negotiate with them again and again. And yet again.

William Ury and Roger Fisher define negotiation as "a back-and-forth communication designed to reach an agreement when you and the other side have some interests that are shared and others that are opposed." Educational resources on the art of negotiating are available in abundance. One can use these techniques in the context of our daily interactions rather than in the business or diplomatic settings most often described in the literature.

The word itself comes from the Latin *negotium*, which is usually translated "business." The Latin root of that word is a combination of *nec,* the negative, and *otium,* meaning idleness, or leisure. In its root meaning, negotiating is "not being idle." It's the opposite of taking it easy. It's getting in there and doing something. In the context of dealing with difficult people, it's a delicate use of our lights and ideas and insights, being receptive to their lights and ideas and insights, affirming what we have in common, then pressing forward to see what we do about our differences.

"Negotiation" has a businesslike ring to it. But the reality of negotiation is in the pervasive daily contacts we have with other people. Normal, stress-free, easy contacts go smoothly enough. It's when we encounter differences of view, differences of intention, of objectives, of personality, that we can turn consciously to negotiation techniques. When we think of our encounters with difficult people as opportunities for nonviolent negotiating, a whole new range of opportunities presents itself. The people with whom we engage in this process don't have to be operating themselves out of the same spirit for us to use negotiation effectively. In fact, they probably won't be. We still, in a spirit of nonviolence, can treat them courteously, respectfully, careful not to let our discourse degenerate.

ACCENTUATE THE POSITIVE

When we engage difficult people in the spirit of nonviolent negotiating, we try to concentrate on the positives, on what we have in common rather than on the differences that divide us. So we don't start out by confronting positions. If we do, our egos quickly become involved and one side becomes determined to win over the other. Fischer and Ury call this "positional bargaining."

> The task of jointly devising an acceptable solution tends to become a battle. Each side tries through sheer willpower to force the other to change its position....Anger and resentment often result as one side sees itself bending to the rigid will of the other while its own legitimate concerns go unaddressed. Positional bargaining thus strains and sometimes shatters the relationship between the parties.

That's why it's been said that, in marriage, "When you win, you lose." When you win a contest of wills, you lose something of the bond that sustains the marriage. The same is true of any other close-knit group of people who have to work together. When one side wins and the other loses, group cohesion is diminished. In nonviolent negotiating, nobody wins until everybody wins.

Negotiation theory suggests that, instead of considering the difference a contest of wills, where I will either defeat them or be defeated by them, we look at the difference as a problem to be solved by us jointly. Instead of you versus me, it's both of us against the problem. *We* together have something to work out. It helps to imagine that, instead of sitting on opposite sides of the table with the problem between us, we are sitting on the same side of the table with the problem in front of us, facing it together. In doing so we rely on the strengths we share to resolve this issue of difference that has come up.

Instead of confrontation, nonviolent negotiating first and often asks "why?" When we find out the reasons for their actions, when we begin to grasp their emotional background, we are then in a position to try, as best we can, to see that the other side understands us.

TRUE LOVE

Love is different from liking. Idiosyncratic personalities may not really like each other, but that doesn't mean they can't love each other. Love is not necessarily a sentiment, feeling good. Love, as Jesus used it, is *agape,* which means personal respect, a firm, committed, clear-eyed intention of wanting what is good for those who, for the moment, are being difficult. This love is not a sentimental feeling that goes against our emotional makeup, something we should try to conjure up in the face of opposition. In looking at difficult people, we shouldn't be stymied by the way we feel. We may feel fearful, disgusted, or antagonistic. Nonviolent love means, first, not letting our differences erupt in destructive behaviors. And then it means searching for what is true and right, which leads to trying to iron out our differences. It means working together, patiently, perseveringly, for their and our genuine good.

The Nonviolent Christ encourages us neither to flee nor to attack defensively. Rather, we are to engage difficult people nonviolently. An acceptable result is our ability to live with them civilly, converse with them respectfully, give help when needed, and accept help graciously. That's the main goal of our loving negotiation. Anything over and above that is gravy.

SEEKING CONSENSUS

Those with whom we work may include some of the difficult people in our lives. Negotiating with them sometimes happens when we are in a group (or that interminable, inescapable group process called a meeting). Nonviolent negotiating seeks to incorporate a process of consensus rather than voting according to the commonly accepted process known as Robert's Rules of Order.

Perhaps I have a subconscious aversion to these Rules because their author, General Henry Martin Robert, was an active duty military officer during the Civil War. But the principal drawback of General Robert's Rules is that they create a process where issues are brought to a vote, with the majority ruling. In this contest, some win and others lose. Those who lose may feel alienated and resentful. Those who win may feel momentarily superior. Gospel Nonviolence does not automatically bless majority rule. Majority rule may be majority tyranny. Majority rule may sacrifice the rights and insights of a minority. Majority rule may be a form of groupthink that sweeps the hesitant in its path and overrides the truth that resides in the minds of those who are outvoted.

Consensus is an alternative decision-making model more compatible with Gandhian nonviolence. The value of the consensus model of decision making is that no one feels left out, everyone's position is heard and given serious consideration. Gospel Nonviolence is based on respect for the basic human dignity of each person. In the consensus process the ideal is the group taking a decision that all agree with. Failing that, it calls for those who disagree after being fully heard to agree to accept the decision as being that of the group, while retaining the right to believe it is not the wisest. Because everyone has been respectfully heard, it is much more difficult to nurse a sense of being defeated and alienated. The process of achieving consensus is the essence of negotiating.

A consensus process can be more time-consuming than a crisp, clear process of motion-second-discussion-vote then go on to the next item. Its value lies in the personal integration in the process and the respect shown to every member of the group. It involves a deliberate effort on the part of the facilitator to elicit everyone's opinion. In the course of the discussion, one member's idea which would have suffered a minority defeat in a vote may, when others hear it and consider it and hash it out, sway the thinking of those who started out with a different idea.

CREATIVE TENSION

What if difficult people refuse to negotiate at all? What if they maintain their position regardless of my overtures, my attempts to get at the reasons for the position, my suggestions for constructive outcomes? What if I'm met with a stubborn insistence on only one outcome—theirs? When that happens, we have the possibility of escalating our opposition so that they see some point to entering into discussion with us. Martin Luther King called it "creative tension." We don't oppose for the sake of opposing, we oppose for the sake of engaging in negotiations.

Several years ago my wife Janice and I were faced with new neighbors in the apartment upstairs. They were pleasant at first, agreeable, cooperative. Unfortunately for us, though, when they completed moving in, they located their sound equipment—television and stereo—in the room directly above our bedroom. Although both were working during the day, they often began the evening with a loud television program or some music with a heavy beat. But the real problem for us was when they played this music or watched a program with the volume high late at night, as we were trying to sleep.

Several times we telephoned them, and they stopped the music. Once we phoned and got no answer. The next morning I called the man at his work. He said he had turned off the ringer of his phone so they wouldn't be disturbed, but he would keep the noise down. But it happened again and again. Powerless to reach them on the phone at home, we got up out of bed one night, went upstairs and knocked on the front door of their apartment. No answer. We knocked louder, and rang the bell. "Creative tension," I'm thinking, hoping they would come to the door, see us bedraggled old folks, and agree to talk about the problem. They didn't.

The next afternoon, Janice went upstairs to talk directly with the woman. She said they had heard us the night before, but decided not to come to the door. She listened to Janice, but didn't respond. It was the man's equipment, she said. She couldn't control it.

He came home from work later that evening. Instead of going upstairs, he came directly to our door. He was upset. His companion had told him about Janice's visit. "Don't you ever talk to her again. I pay the bills, I make the decisions. And, also, don't ever call me at work again."

Aha, we thought, negotiations begin. Creative tension worked. We are now talking.

We tried to keep our voices level, non-accusatory. It was hard. We wanted to give him the chance to ventilate his frustration at our desire to interfere with his auditory pleasure. This was the first time he had lived away from home. When we told him how the music and especially the television were keeping us awake at night, he responded, "You sound just like my mother." He reiterated his position: he paid the rent, he had the right to do whatever he wanted in his apartment. We suggested the possibility of a ten to seven moratorium on loud music, he rejected it completely. He was going to do whatever he wanted. We should stay out of his way.

We were not going to fall into the trap of positional bargaining, of a contest of wills. But it was hard. Finally, Janice said, injecting a bit of creative tension again, "You talk like you don't care one bit about us." He was taken aback. He said, "Yes, I do. But I'm not going to change my life because of you." We realized the conversation had gone about as far as it could go. Nonviolent negotiation suggests knowing when to quit. We quit, for the time being.

However, the outcome was entirely different from his closing words. In fact, the loud music and television playing stopped at night, almost entirely. Once in a while, in the morning, he would turn it up, but hardly ever at night any more. When we saw him outside, we thanked him for his thoughtfulness. Although our Gandhian negotiation had not produced a verbal apology and a firm purpose of amendment, it did have the desired results: quiet nights. We put up with the music during the day, he kept it down, for the most part, at night.

Several months later, he moved out, informing us he had bought a house. Apartment living apparently was not for him. The neighbors who replaced him were models of considerateness.

Because we human beings are not always consistent, not always clear-headed, not always wise, not always altruistic, our nonviolent negotiations, whether with individuals or in groups, are going to be chancy. What we can say with confidence, though, is that in the spirit of the Nonviolent Christ, they're the way to go.

QUESTIONS FOR REFLECTION AND DISCUSSION

1. Is "negotiation" a helpful image for dealing with difficult people, or is it distracting? Can you think of other images?

2. What truth is there in the suggestion that, in a conflict with someone with whom you have a close relation, "when you win, you lose"?

3. How is it possible to *love* a difficult person without *liking* the person?

4. Those organized gatherings called "meetings" are a growing fact of life for most of us. What advantage does a consensus model for reaching decisions have over a voting model?

5. Can you think of ways of introducing a little "creative tension" into a negotiation that is proving stubborn?

CHAPTER TEN

In the dictionary of satyagraha *there is no "enemy."*

—Gandhi

SURVIVING OUR ENEMIES

Because our efforts to organize the Compassionate Commonwealth will meet with opposition, we have to be prepared to face opposition and try to turn it around. Gandhi's nonviolent dictionary did not include "enemy" because the image of "enemy" conjures up implacable hostility. Gandhi wanted no one to live with implacable hostility. His *satyagraha* pointed in a different direction.

Enemies are individuals or groups who for whatever reason want to hurt us seriously. They come in many shapes and forms. A person who jumps out in the dark to attack with a weapon is at that moment an enemy. Agents of a foreign power who send missiles to wreak havoc are enemies on a larger scale, even though they may have nothing against us personally.

When I think "enemy," I shudder. I hate the thought of realizing that there may be people out there who want to do serious damage to me or my loved ones. I may have offended them in some way. My public positions may have alienated some, threatened others. A friend of ours, active in the Civil Rights Movement of the 1960s, received an anonymous card in the mail. On the front was a drawing of the cross hairs of a gun. Inside were printed words: "Beware of the milkman, the paper boy, the postman, you don't know who, but the cross hairs are on the back of your neck." She admitted being afraid.

The country of which I'm a citizen certainly has made enemies by supporting dictators, bolstering oppressive regimes. However justified our enemies might be, the thought of them makes me afraid. And that fear makes me want to do what most of us feel like doing in the face of enemies, flight or fight. Get away from them, ignore them, even pretend they don't exist. Or fight back. Be ready to defend against them, maybe even launch a preemptive strike. So many of us learned in childhood to fight back physically when we were threatened.

From the Nonviolent Christ we have a third alternative. "You have heard that it was said, 'You shall love your neighbor and hate your enemy.' But I say to you, love your enemies, and pray for those who persecute you" (Matthew 5:43–44).

A word of caution, however, before we gird ourselves to meet enemies in Jesus' nonviolent way. We need to make sure they are *real* enemies, that we're not just imagining their hostility. It's easy to extrapolate hostile intentions from a slight or a careless word. It's easy to engage in "enemy-think." It's easy to suspect that people are hostile, especially if we don't know them very well. And what a sad mistake it is to imagine that someone or some group is hostile when they really aren't. *Satyagraha* calls us to the firm pursuit of truth, of seeing what really is and acting on that, rather than relying on vague suspicions that stem more from our own shadow than from the flesh and blood human beings we're facing.

INTERNATIONAL ENEMIES

The Nonviolent Christ would have us look on our country's enemies in a different way than Pentagon planners do. The latter have been given a mission to be alert to potential dangers from foreign forces who would threaten our country's vital interests. Identifying those potential enemies then leads to planning military defenses. It's the "fight" response, never the flight. It means having enough weapons and trained personnel and strategic deployment to cause considerable damage to those enemies should their threat lead to hostile action. To do so the government needs a continued flow of large sums of money.

In the late years of the 1990s, the Pentagon had its eyes on what one military officer called the Six Demon Nations—Iran, Iraq, Libya, Syria, North Korea, and Cuba. These were the countries expected to be most hostile to the United States, most likely to do something harmful to our interests, the ones we needed to be prepared to go to war against at a moment's notice. But even from a cold, military viewpoint, none of these nations posed a drastic danger to the United States. The Center for Defense Information pointed out:

> Cuba cannot be taken seriously as a threat. Other proposed threats are balanced by strong neighbors. Syria, for example, is militarily inferior to Israel and faces Turkey and Iraq on its other borders. Libya is far weaker than Egypt. Iran remains counterbalanced by Iraq and is technologically inferior to Saudi Arabia and other Gulf states, particularly in the key area of air power.

So what's going on here? Gospel Nonviolence calls us to be suspicious of such enemy listings. It creates an imperative for us to investigate more closely, to take a long, hard look at this whole process. Why the emphasis on military means to counter supposed enemies, even if they are real and not just a figment of financial or career needs? Why not, instead, an emphasis on international cooperation, on diplomacy instead of weapons? Why not, indeed?

Something unsavory is afoot. Enemies reinforce a righteous national self-image. That, in turn, keeps us from examining our national conduct to see if we've done anything to provoke the hostility (if it really exists). It also hinders us from expending national energy in solving problems at home in favor of concentrating on enemies abroad. Even citizens of Nazi Germany put aside the possibility of internal reform when faced with an Allied enemy bent on destroying them. So did the Stalinist Soviet Union. They rallied around the cause of defending their territory when it was under attack.

The Nonviolent Christ would point us in a different direction: seek constructive engagements, develop positive programs that would serve the interests of the people, especially those who are least able to take care of themselves.

REAL ENEMIES

Although the word "enemy" may not be in Gandhi's dictionary, it occurs sixteen times in the gospels. Jesus was realistic in acknowledging the existence of enemies. They're out there, all right. What Jesus did was teach a radically different way of acting toward them, different from the usual responses of getting away or striking back. Jesus was not expressing an impossible ideal, but rather showing a way of genuine, effective power, the power to defuse enmity and move toward a spirit of reconciliation.

Because in real life it's so difficult to love those who are out to hurt us, Jesus' enemy-love is the acid test of his commandment to love neighbors as we love ourselves. We don't have to *like* them, we just have to *love* them in the sense of wanting what is good for them. What's good for them, right now, is for them to stop wanting to hurt me. But how in the world do we get them to stop?!

"Christ gave us the spirit," King said, "and Gandhi showed us the method." Gandhi's *satyagraha* shows us how to put Jesus' enemy love to work. Abraham Lincoln's image is helpful: "I destroy my enemies when I make them my friends." Enemy-love, acting through Gandhian nonviolence, can—although not easily and not quickly—turn enemies into friends. The Nonviolent Christ encourages us to engage enemies nonviolently with all the techniques and tactics that have been developed over decades and centuries of nonviolent living. The ideal result is that our enemies become our friends. That's what it will be like in the City of God, the Compassionate Commonwealth. That's when nobody's dictionary will contain the word "enemy." We move in that direction when we use our repertoire of nonviolent techniques in meeting the opposition of those who would hurt us.

PERSONAL ASSAULT

In a climate of intensifying violence, we are most likely to encounter real, live, in-our-face enemies in the form of a mugging, a robbery, a threatened attack on our person. This is where our dedication to following the Nonviolent Christ receives its most stringent test. How will we respond? What can we do now to prepare ourselves to respond nonviolently before an attack actually happens?

With the increasing possibility of personal assault, we can enhance our chances of survival through sound preparation consisting of prevention, self-possession, and practicing nonviolent responses in less threatening encounters.

Prevention involves using normal caution to avoid potentially dangerous places and times. It includes locking doors, walking to one's car with someone else, avoiding dark, unfamiliar places. *Self-possession* means refusing to act like a victim, appearing confident. It involves having a sense of direction, a feeling of self-possession, and carrying oneself in a way that exudes these qualities. Convicted assaulters say they can spot a potential target, a "vic," by the way the person seems hesitant, insecure, afraid. One sure sign of a victim is to beg the attacker not to do it, to stop. That's almost always counterproductive. It feeds the attacker's sense of being in command.

The third area of preparation is to employ deliberate nonviolent responses in less threatening conflicts, like with the "difficult" people in our life. When we find ourselves in an argument, we can consciously remember not to fight back in kind, not to give an eye for an eye, not to argue our position in a way that humiliates our opponent. We don't provoke, we don't counterattack. We attempt carefully to establish some kind of personal rapport, so that the spark of decency at the heart of everyone can have the opportunity to emerge and counter the energy of opposition.

But, in spite of our best preventive efforts, a physical assault may come. It's a fearsome prospect. It may erupt suddenly, without warning, a stranger appearing out of nowhere, striking, knocking us down, grabbing at purse or chain or ring, perhaps firing shots at us. Hit and run. There's really nothing we can do to ward off such a sudden invasion of our personal space. Even someone carrying a weapon couldn't use it against a lightning fast assault. Following the Nonviolent Christ, we wouldn't have the weapon option. But neither could we employ any nonviolent techniques in a quick encounter. Sometimes, the attack is so sudden, so swift, so effective that only one response is possible: to forgive our assailant—as Pope John Paul II forgave Mehmet Ali Agca, as Cardinal Joseph Bernardin did his emotional enemy Steven Cook, who falsely accused him of sexual molestation. We could only ask, as Jesus did on the cross, "Father, forgive them, they know not what they do" (Luke 23:34).

But, most often, there will be a little time or distance between us and the intruder, giving us the opportunity to engage nonviolently. If we can see a threatening person approaching, or if the assailant begins by speaking, by asking or demanding our wallet, purse, money, or by pushing us around, we have an opportunity for nonviolent intervention. We can keep calm, attempt to engage in some way to establish a human, personal link. When Angie O'Gorman woke up to the crash of her bedroom door being kicked open and found a strange man at the foot of her bed, she looked right at him and said, "What time is it?" When he fumbled for his watch to reply, she engaged him in what later seemed a surreal conversation about whether his watch or her bedside clock had the correct time. But it was enough to lower the level of his hostility after engaging her as a person in a verbal exchange.

This kind of nonviolent resistance takes courage. It is not for the fainthearted. It's for those who realize their own substantial personal power. It does not mean, out of some misguided sense of love or fear of offending, that we let people run over us. Rather, we should do something positive. If it's positive and unexpected, but nonthreatening, it will throw the enemy off balance, and likely cause the enemy to pause. Richard Gregg called it *moral jiu-jitsu*. It's also been called "throwing a curve." It's what Gandhi did in organizing the Salt March to the Sea. It's what King did in allowing children to take part in demonstrations in Birmingham, when the world was shocked by scenes of police dogs and fire hoses sweeping away neatly dressed and politely behaved young people. It's what Allen Ginsberg did when he was mugged in Central Park. "Sure, I'll give you my money. But first let's go have a cup of coffee so you can tell me why you need the money." When enemies are momentarily taken aback, they have a chance to change. They may even be be embarrassed by their aggression. If so, their embarrassment would be the "burning coals" which Paul said would be heaped on our enemies' heads if we fed them when they were hungry, helped them in their true need.

A First Time

I used to be able to say I haven't been mugged, yet. Now I can't say that. It happened one sultry Memphis evening in 1996. After dinner at home with a friend, Janice and I walked him to his car in the parking area near our apartment. He had just bought a new car. Janice got in the driver's seat to admire it. Two young men sauntered over, young men like many others who lived in our apartment complex. Suddenly one of them spoke. "Give me your wallet." The other had a gun, a shiny chrome automatic, pointing in our direction. I said I didn't have my wallet with me. Our friend began reaching in his pocket for his. Janice, sitting in the car, heard "wallet," and thought these two young people were just harassing us. She didn't see the gun. She called out from the car, in her best schoolteacher voice, "Go away, stop bothering us, just leave. Right now!" The two young men looked at her, startled, glanced back at us as though trying to figure out what to do. Then they turned and ran away as fast as I've ever seen anyone run. The whole event lasted less than a minute. Janice had "thrown a curve" for which they were totally unprepared. It saved a wallet, and maybe more.

Followers of the Nonviolent Christ have the mental upper hand in a threatened assault, because we know the assailant's mind better than the assailant knows ours. We know that those bent on hurting us are themselves hurting in some way. They may be in financial desperation, not out to do bodily harm, but just to take our money. They expect, by threatening us, that we'll do what they want—hand it over.

Their hurt may be deeper, an emotional wound they subconsciously want to counter by making us feel as bad as they do. But, as our working hypothesis, we have what the poet Longfellow observed: "If we could read the secret history of our enemies, we should find in each [one's] life sorrow and suffering enough to disarm all hostility."

We know they're hurting in some way, even though they may not show it. We also know that they're afraid. They have no idea what we'll do when they attack, whether we have a weapon for defense or a magic whistle to summon immediate assistance. They may act tough, authoritative, demanding, in charge, supported by their weaponry. But inside, they are hurting and they are fearful. We are in a much better emotional state than they are. While knowing this does not guarantee a favorable outcome to the encounter, it does significantly increase our nonviolent chances.

The Nonviolent Christ does not promise 100% success in defusing real enemies as the world terms success—escaping unharmed with possessions intact. We are only promised that our fidelity in trying to love them is in harmony with the deepest secrets of the Universe, and that it will help rather than hinder the development of the Compassionate Commonwealth.

QUESTIONS FOR REFLECTION AND DISCUSSION

1. How can you tell a *real* enemy from one that is just *imagined?*

2. Who is the current front and center Demon Nation right now? What do you know about that nation?

3. How might it be possible for that Demon Nation to be transformed into a friendly or at least neutral international player?

4. In the present culture of violence, chances of being subject to personal assault are growing. What preventive measures are you taking to lessen the chances for yourself?

5. How can walking the way of the Nonviolent Christ help you survive the very real enemy who assaults you?

CHAPTER ELEVEN

I imagine a world where abortion is unthinkable.

—Shelley Douglass

PRO LIFE—ALL LIFE

The words about abortion have all been spoken. The positions have been outlined, the stands taken. The abortion debate is over. There is no need to rehash the arguments. It's up to each one to see where we find our place in the spectrum that ranges from the total moral condemnation of all abortion, to the complete acceptance of even partial birth abortion should it be the pregnant woman's decision.

The reality, as we're about to enter the twenty-first century, is that abortion is legal almost everywhere in the world. Here and there certain conditions restrict legal access to it, conditions that are more or less stringent. Although individuals may be divided on whether it is right or wrong, moral or immoral, abortion is undeniably a part of world culture. And that's not about to change, no matter how passionately anti-abortion advocates express their opposition.

What is also a part of world culture, unfortunately, is the lack of widespread support and understanding for a woman facing a problem pregnancy and looking for a way out other than abortion. She may be young and single, exposed from childhood to overt expressions of sexuality. She may find herself involved in a sexual incident, maybe willingly, maybe not, maybe haphazardly. If she becomes pregnant, she suddenly faces another aspect of her culture, its disapproval of her pregnancy. She realizes she is expected to "take care of it," become un-pregnant, get back to a "normal" existence. Abortion is easy, it's legal, it's available. She feels pressured to take advantage of it. Whatever the emotional aftermath, it will be hers alone to deal with. She got herself caught between two pressures, one sexual and permissive, the other disapproving of her unmarried pregnancy. She has to cope as best she can.

Another woman may be married, with children already, then becomes pregnant again. She has a serious health problem that in all probability will kill her if she carries her pregnancy through to term. Yet another woman may live in a part of the world that values male babies more highly than females, and learns through amniocentesis that the fetus she is carrying will be another girl rather than the boy her husband fervently wants. So she has an abortion rather than kill the baby girl after it is born.

PART-TIME CONVICTIONS

I confess to being distressed by those who claim to be pro-life in the matter of abortion, but who favor war and the death penalty and personal guns. I am uneasy when someone passionately opposes abortion, but approves of government threats to kill large numbers of innocents through weapons of mass destruction, killing that Gordon Zahn called "post-natal abortion."

> The [person] who somehow finds it possible to maintain an olympian silence in the face of government policies which contemplate the destruction of human life on a massive scale, has no right to issue indignant protests when the same basic disregard for human life is given expression in government policies permitting or encouraging abortion.

I find a certain split-mindedness in those who would have the state declare abortion illegal in the interest of preserving life, but who would have the same state kill people convicted of serious crimes and attempt to justify it on some grounds other than sheer revenge.

I am also disturbed by those sensitive to other life issues who seem to have a blind eye concerning the taking of human life before birth, those who insist that it's not human life but the "product of conception," or a "fertilized ovum," or simply a growth inside the body similar to a wart or a tumor on the outside, or those who admit that it's the beginning of human life but believe that the mother's right to decide takes precedence over that nascent life.

Both sides contain a fair number of adherents who express a fanaticism which for a long time I found puzzling. This is a fanaticism that leads some pro-lifers to burn abortion clinics, physically abuse those assisting in abortions, and emphatically affirm that stopping abortion ought to be everyone's top priority. Pro-choice fanaticism calls shrilly for abortion on demand, decries all restrictions as male brutality, and dismisses as irrelevant any concern over the complexity of the question.

LISTEN TO THE WOMEN

I was able to get a better handle on this fanaticism when I began paying much closer attention to the voices of women on the subject of abortion than the opinions of men. Men can ponder, men can pontificate, men can be logically persuasive. But men cannot be pregnant. As I listened to the women, I began to get a feel for what else is at stake besides a decision to terminate a pregnancy and end a developing human life.

I heard advocates of abortion putting the issue in the larger context of the liberation of women from eons of male domination, especially sexual domination. Sally Miller Gearhart is one such voice. She believes that abortion is an important way women can free themselves:

> The whole of feminism in these last two centuries has been concerned with the liberation of women from their role as sexual servants of men...Guarantee [all women] freedom from rape, from battering, from genital mutilation, from the sexual slavery that keeps the traffic in women a thriving global business...Release women from the economic dependency upon men that requires them to say "yes" to a sex act, whether as wife or prostitute.

Leah Fritz sees abortion as "an act of responsibility" for thousands of women caught in the crushing circumstances of poverty or rape. She reacts strongly against *men* who would deprive women of that right.

In the context of the real world, abortion is a life-saving procedure most often resorted to by mothers of living children who must limit the size of their families in order to provide for them. But there are many other valid life-sustaining and life-enhancing reasons to end an unwanted pregnancy...The random accident of union between sperm and egg often occurs under unholy conditions, namely rape, incest, and seduction...It is categorically immoral for men to play on the conditioned selflessness of women by urging them to give greater consideration of the "viability" of embryos than to their own valuable lives and futures.

These voices are heard as threatening by many, both men and women. Many men feel a loss of balance as they realize that the world where they were assumed to be superior is gone and will never return. Overturning of the male-dominated world has been accompanied by a sexual revolution where conduct previously unacceptable became more overt. Sexual experimentation, living together before marriage, and same-sex liaisons are taken for granted in the current climate, although tempered by a new anxiety, the AIDS epidemic. Some women, too, who have learned to maneuver competently in this new world are unsure what exactly is demanded of them. The sands are shifting, the footing is uncertain.

The same burst of energy that produced the push for women's equality also produced a racial revolution. People formerly subjected to secondary roles emerged as fully equal, sometimes superior, demanding and getting places heretofore reserved for white males. In the dismay at all this turmoil, at changes that eroded a sense of place and purpose, it was easy to focus on the legalization of abortion, which took effect in the United States with the Supreme Court decision of 1973. Many, both men and women, who favor racial equality, women's liberation from male domination, and greater sexual freedom, had misgivings over the virtually unlimited lifting of restrictions on abortion, viewing it as another element in the decay of moral values, another victory for the culture of violence. The near fanaticism on one side or the other of the abortion question is rooted in these other issues. Pro-life, pro-choice—that's on the surface. Under the surface is deep perplexity, uncertainty, anxiety over the deeper currents in our common enterprise called life.

One woman's voice that I find very persuasive, though, is that of Shelley Douglass, wife, mother, peace activist, hostess of a Catholic Worker house. She has devoted her life to helping bring about a climate of respect and mutual support. Her vision is:

> ...a world of peace, where it's assumed that everybody will be sustained at a basic level, not a world where some people will be floating in superfluous wealth and other people starving. A peaceful world, where there are other ways of solving conflicts than killing each other, a world where rape was also unthinkable, and where economics did not force women into sexual activity. I think, if we were able to create a world where those were the assumptions, it would go a long way toward a world where abortion wouldn't happen...In our society as it is now abortions are going to happen. The real question, it seems to me, is the question of the struggle for liberation for people, all people, but especially women, to be able to make choices in their lives, to be supported by their society, to be respected and allowed to become full persons.

Shelley Douglass is describing the Compassionate Commonwealth. Although we may be keeping our eyes on that prize and working to bring it about, we're far away from accomplishing it, so far that it's barely a distant glimmer on the horizon, a glimmer that might even be a mirage. We're slogging through the mud of the present culture of violence. In the present here and now, governments embrace policies of mass murder through sophisticated weaponry, policies of assassinating "enemy" agents, policies of executing citizens declared guilty of certain crimes, all for the purpose of defending what the governments have declared vital interests at home and abroad. The same governments have caused other innocents to stumble into poverty, homelessness, and hunger because of the enormous amount of resources dedicated to maintaining the machinery of death. In this atmosphere of trivialization of human life after birth, it is very easy, a "no-brainer" to accept the termination of human life before birth.

The Catholic bishops of the United States as a body are on record deploring some aspects of this culture of violence.

Increasingly, our society looks to violent measures to deal with some of our most difficult social problems—millions of abortions to address problem pregnancies, advocacy of euthanasia and assisted suicide to cope with the burdens of age and illness, and increased reliance on the death penalty to deal with crime...A society which destroys its children, abandons its old, and relies on vengeance fails fundamental moral tests...How do we teach the young to curb their violence when we embrace it as the solution to social problems?

The answer, obviously, is that our society doesn't teach anybody, young or old, to curb their violence. Rather, it teaches that violence, including abortion, is an acceptable means to remove threatening obstacles or to achieve one's goals.

OUR WAY

That's the way of the world. The way of the Nonviolent Christ involves two clear attitudes: respect for all life, including preborn, and compassion for women undergoing problem pregnancies in the vestiges of a male-dominated society. The taking of any life, before or after birth, is to be infinitely regretted. There is no such thing as the "good" killing of human beings. There is no morally good violence.

This is a *moral* judgment. It needs to be kept distinct from the *legal* question of whether or not abortion should be made a criminal offense. In the Compassionate Commonwealth, citizens would be bolstered by a legal system in which all taking of human life is beyond the pale, and provisions would be in place to give abundant assistance to all pregnant women. In our present imperfect world, characterized all too often by the lack of such compassionate concern, to advocate laws against abortion is in effect to back women into desperate corners. It would force many into seeking dangerous illegal abortions, and some into suicidal despair.

I agree with the pro-life stance of Pax Christi-USA, the Catholic Peace Movement. Pax Christi rejects war and war preparations, capital punishment, and all other forms of violence, while expressing compassion for all who suffer from any of these. I especially respect its position on abortion because the voices of women were clear and strong in formulating it:

> Our concern must not only ensure saving the lives of the not-yet-born but also include recognizing that every child must be assured the opportunity to meet their basic human needs and to develop and fulfill their physical, intellectual and spiritual capacities...We must recognize that women who are considering abortion often struggle with a complex and painful dilemma. We must ensure that women do not choose abortion because of a lack of economic assistance, child care, health care or emotional support. No matter what decision is reached, they should be received with loving concern and compassion by the followers of Christ.

Perhaps it's time now for *men* to step back, and yield center stage in the matter of abortion to women, for whom abortion is a matter of direct, personal concern in a way that it can never be for men. This is not a call for evasion of responsibility. It is a call for appropriate humility. What all of us can do, men and women, with the Nonviolent Christ, the Good Shepherd, is to speak tenderly to all pregnant women, give comfort and all possible help as they grapple with the painful alternatives thrust upon them.

QUESTIONS FOR REFLECTION AND DISCUSSION

1. Where do you personally stand on the abortion issue?

2. List the social pressures favoring abortion as a solution to a problem pregnancy.

3. Do you know abortion opponents, pro-life people, who favor capital punishment and support the nation's wars? How do they deal with the apparent inconsistency in their position?

4. What weight do you give to the voices of the women quoted in this chapter (pp. 84-87)?

5. In the Compassionate Commonwealth, how would a problem pregnancy be treated?

The God of life summons us to life; more, to be lifegivers, especially toward those who lie under the heel of the powers.

—Daniel Berrigan

NONVIOLENT CONFRONTATION

*C*onfronting a Culture of Violence was the title of a 1994 Pastoral Message of the U.S. Catholic Bishops. *Confronting* is a strong word. The Pastoral Message did not ask people to "live with" a culture of violence, or "be resigned" to it, or even "endure" it. Nor did the message merely advise "trying to change it." The controlling image was *confronting* the culture of violence. Confront means to face something squarely, in a challenging mode. Confront means to *oppose* it actively. The word evokes a medieval image of confronting a possessed person with a crucifix. Someone writhing in demonic possession was confronted by a crucifix held by an exorcist, in the belief that the crucified Christ could banish the power of Satan. And it often worked. Many people diagnosed as being possessed were healed.

Confrontation involves challenge. We challenge something when we call it into question, when we suggest boldly that it is outmoded, out of date, or downright unjust. That's what we do when in the spirit of the Nonviolent Christ we confront the culture of violence. We're convinced that it's outmoded, indeed downright unjust, and we show our conviction by the way we live. We challenge the culture of violence when we ourselves act in the certainty that violence is no longer acceptable, that it's tired and outdated no matter how many cling to it in the stubborn belief that it still works and that it's still valid.

But that's their time lag, that's their dragging along in the past, that's their acceptance of a social disease that has felled millions, that, like an epidemic, rages and subsides and rages again, but for which a cure is at hand. The cure is active nonviolence. It's a different way of living, a way that works, a way that's right, a way that's in harmony with the Cosmos, a way that provides us with personal spiritual integrity.

The Nonviolent Christ offers the cure by showing, first, the reality of violence for what it is, by unmasking it as a violation of human dignity and decency no matter what justifications are offered for it. And then he provides, especially with his enemy-love, a way for everyone to turn down the spiral of violence in their own lives. When we come to the conviction that this is a way that works for us, we know that it can work for everyone else, too.

Then we enter in to the long, patient effort of communicating it, of helping others understand that yes there is a cure for the social cancer of violence, no we don't have to be its victims, all of us can do something about it, and it's in the best interest of everyone to undergo the cure. We confront the culture of violence when we communicate the antidote of nonviolence.

The first way we confront the culture of violence is in our own personal lives, by attempting to live our daily interactions in a consciously nonviolent way. We confront the culture of violence by the nonviolent way we deal with "difficult" people, by the way we approach conflicts in a spirit of negotiation rather than dominance, by the respect we show to those with whom we disagree, by closing doors softly and sensitively in the intimacy of our own families, by the careful way we use words, by promising only what we can fulfill and by fulfilling whatever we promise.

Although the 1994 Pastoral Message did not advocate a commitment to active nonviolence as the overall framework for confronting the culture of violence, it did suggest other immediate personal ways of living out that confrontation:

> Perhaps the greatest challenge is the call for all of us to examine our own lives, to identify how we can choose generosity over selfishness, and choose a real commitment to family and community over individual acquisition and ambition. In many small ways, each of us can help overcome violence by dealing with it on our block; providing for the emotional, physical, and spiritual needs of our children; dealing with our own abusive behavior; or even treating fellow motorists with courtesy. Violence is overcome day by day, choice by choice, person by person. All of us must make a contribution.

Besides the choices we make to live more nonviolently in our personal lives, at times we may decide to confront the culture of violence in its war-making stance with the more dramatic actions of pouring blood, blockading entrances to military installations, witnessing publicly in front of plants engaged in manufacturing instruments of death. Eventually, if we are faithful to the Nonviolent Christ, we will be disruptive of the status quo. And rightly so, because the status quo is a status of violence. At times we will be seen as troublemakers, agitators, subversives. But so was the Nonviolent Christ.

Whichever emphasis we give at any particular time, our model in confronting the culture of violence is the Nonviolent Christ, crucified and risen, the One who has already overcome death, "who destroyed death and brought life and immortality to light through the gospel" (2 Timothy 1:10). Confident that his Spirit shows us the way, we can display the spirit of the Nonviolent Christ in our own lives, and do it in a manner that conveys thoughtful conviction more than innocent naivete. Some may think us fools for Christ, but if we show that we really know what we're doing, that we've examined the alternatives and historical precedents and are familiar with the immediate mechanics, their dismissal becomes an indictment of their own naivete.

THE COOPERATION OPTION

Our confrontation with the culture of violence will itself be non-violent. We won't attempt to force our way down anyone's throat. We may be convinced that violence is always wrong, and that nonviolent means are always better. But we best confront the culture of violence most of the time by our gentle witness, although at times a stronger, more public push is necessary—to oppose an imminent outbreak of war, for example. The Nonviolent Christ encourages us to go easy on absolutizing. He discourages us from ideological imperialism, from attempting to convince everyone that our way is superior to theirs and that they had better get with it or else. The Nonviolent Christ has not given us a new _law_ of nonviolence. Jesus' only _law_ is the law of love: "I give you a new commandment: love one another. As I have loved you, so you also should love one another" (John 13:34). That's the only commandment. We may see nonviolence as an extension of that commandment, but most people resigned to the culture of violence won't. We express nonviolence much more attractively when we do not expound it as a definitive mandate that binds and forces others where they would not now go, but hold it as a vision of how best to act in a violent world.

This is especially true when we interact with those who are sincerely trying to confront injustice and don't see any way to do so without resorting to force. The debate that emerged in the late 1960s over the possibility of a just revolution brought out sincere supporters of both sides. Many enthusiastic, would-be builders of the City of God, justly indignant because of violent structures they saw oppressing so many of God's people, especially in Latin America, openly advocated overthrowing those structures with revolutionary violence. Those who maintained that only a nonviolent approach was appropriate disagreed, sometimes heatedly. The Nonviolent Christ shows us that we should identify with the cause of justice but not with the tactics of violence. But we should be careful not to insist, from a perch of privilege, that they either rebel nonviolently or not at all. Ched Myers put it this way:

Violence is always wrong...This may be our conviction, but we should be aware that this categorical approach...tends to antagonize those trying to confront injustice concretely...particularly when articulated from a privileged First World site...We are hypocritical to suggest nonviolence to those in dangerous and difficult situations we have not ourselves experienced.

UNIVERSAL LOYALTY

We also confront the culture of violence by being appreciative of those who look different, who speak a different language, who profess a different faith, who live under a different economic system. Violence is individualistic, disruptive. We confront it by showing an awareness of global interconnectedness. It was no coincidence that the early years of the Nuclear Age were the time when Gandhian nonviolence took root in the Civil Rights Movement in the United States. Thoughtful people had begun to realize that Hiroshima ushered in not only an era of terrifying new weaponry, but also a new morality of universalism. The Nuclear Age was bringing about for the first time the ability to destroy everyone on the planet. It was creating new links of horror and possibility beyond every political boundary. Already the first bombs were spawning genetic defects in the next generation. Hiroshima and Nagasaki were giving impetus to an arms race that produced an ever expanding supply of technologically sophisticated weapons. Tribe and nation, primary concepts before Hiroshima, were becoming insufficient centers of loyalty. Hiroshima, with its implication of transnational annihilation, demanded an identification with all of humanity. It forced on people the world over the realization that we are one family with one destiny. It demanded that our ultimate loyalty must be to the entire human community, and not just to our own intimate associations. Martin Luther King's nonviolent Civil Rights Movement tapped into this universal loyalty. It helped thoughtful people move beyond the bounds of their own racial community. Our aim in building the Compassionate Commonwealth is a community that will embrace *all* peoples of the world, beyond *all* boundaries of race and creed and national identity.

When we approach others in the spirit of respecting their lights rather than pressing ours on them, more often than not we will experience a pleasant surprise. They will relax, and look at us with new respect. Gospel Nonviolence strikes a responsive chord deep inside. The cure is actually a relief. Most people would prefer to be nonviolent most of the time. Most people try to work things out with those with whom they disagree before resorting to force. Most prefer to sidestep unpleasantness, and direct efforts to healing rather than hurting. But sometimes people find themselves in situations where a nonviolent alternative does not seem to present itself. Then, when things get tough, they act as the culture has taught them to act. They become violent.

We know, because of the Nonviolent Christ, that the human race has survived because of cooperation, not competition. As Gandhi said, nonviolence is a law of our species. Secure in this conviction, we carry on nonviolently even when caught up in the turmoil of disturbance. Our calm in the face of fury is a way of confronting the culture in a nonviolent way.

As we engage in confronting the culture of violence, we are simultaneously constructing the Compassionate Commonwealth, the new City where "tears are turned into dancing." We are actively engaged in *peace*-making. Peace is *an environment where conflicts are resolved without violence, where people are free, not exploited, living so they can grow to their full potential.* It is, in Bishop Carroll Dozier's words, "a gift as well as a task," God's promise as well as our responsibility. All our actions of nonviolent confrontation—personal conviction, patient interaction, firm disagreement, loving service—can be linked to making real, here and now, some aspect of that peace which is the overriding characteristic of the Compassionate Commonwealth.

But peace is evanescent, it's changing, it's flowing. To resolve a conflict without violence today doesn't mean the conflict will stay resolved tomorrow. Even if we know techniques of nonviolent conflict resolution, we may not be able to put those techniques into practice the next time we're faced with a conflict.

And even if we master those techniques, many others haven't, so conflicts will continue to swirl and people will react with some new kind of violence. We are constantly faced with the challenge of confronting a culture of violence. Peace-making is a process, a never-ending engagement, always a new challenge.

Paul wrote, "Whatever you do, whether in speech or in action, do it in the name of Jesus our Savior" (Colossians 3:17*). Today this means, concretely, whatever we do, in our speech or in our action, do everything in light of the City of God, the Kingdom of Heaven, the Compassionate Commonwealth. Trying to live with the Nonviolent Christ gives us no grounds for complacency.

HOPE

In the vision of the New Jerusalem from the book of Revelation, we have the comforting assurance that our nonviolent dream is not an impossible one. The New Jerusalem, a symbol for the Compassionate Commonwealth, will be the final and definitive outcome of creation.

> I also saw a new Jerusalem, the holy City, coming down out of heaven from God, beautiful as a bride and groom on their wedding day. And I heard a loud voice calling from the throne, "Look! God's tabernacle is among humanity! God will live with them; they will be God's people, and God will be fully present among them. The Most High will wipe away every tear from their eyes. And death, mourning, crying and pain will be no more, for the old order has fallen (Revelation 21:2–4*).

As we enter the twenty-first century, we are buoyed by confidence that the power implicit in the gospel and renewed by Gandhi and King and a host of others has been brought to new life with the Nonviolent Christ. We find hope in the growing willingness to confront the culture of violence, the basic decency of people coming to the fore, the deep desire to create a more wholesome atmosphere in which to live and move and have our being.

QUESTIONS FOR REFLECTION AND DISCUSSION

1. "We confront the culture of violence when we communicate the antidote of nonviolence" (p. 91). How can we communicate the antidote of nonviolence in our own personal lives?

2. How can we communicate the antidote of nonviolence in our lives as citizens?

3. How can we communicate the antidote of nonviolence with those who seriously disagree with us?

4. The Nuclear Age has helped us to see that our loyalty extends beyond family and friends, beyond national boundaries, to include people everywhere. Can you imagine an instance where your loyalties would conflict? What would the Nonviolent Christ have you do in such an instance?

5. Where do you find personal hope in the midst of the culture of violence?

PART THREE

OUR BEST INTEREST

One day we shall win freedom, but not only for ourselves. We shall so appeal to your heart and conscience that we shall win *you* in the process, and our victory will be a double victory.

—Martin Luther King

CHAPTER THIRTEEN

*When I have money, I get rid of it quickly, lest it find a way
into my heart.* —John Wesley

NONVIOLENT MONEY

A peace activist friend said the phrase "nonviolent money" seemed to him an oxymoron. He was thinking of money's worldwide status: exploitation of the many poor by the few wealthy, unconscionable waste of tax monies on weapons of war, the pillage of nature impelled by greed for profits. The linking of the words "nonviolent" and "money" seemed an outlandish combination.

Money itself is neither violent nor nonviolent. People are. What's at stake in "nonviolent money" are ways people striving to be nonviolent look at money, deal with money, need it, get it, spend it, withhold it, give it away. A nonviolent perspective on money recognizes its necessity, acknowledges its danger, and seeks a wise way to use it.

MONEY IS NECESSARY

Given the present makeup of contemporary society, money is an obtrusive fact of life. It wasn't always so. For ages people bartered, traded goods for services. But with the advent of a common medium of exchange, money became necessary to supply one's needs. A few continued to be self-sustaining by living off fruits and berries, cultivating land, husbanding the seeds supplied by nature, constructing shelter from palm fronds, and continually recycling all so that nature's abundance would be renewed. But the vast majority of people don't live that way. For us, the medium we call money is necessary to purchase food, buy or rent shelter, obtain clothes and transportation and education, and to supply similar necessities for those who depend on us.

Constant decisions about money are thrust on us, whether we like it or not. If we don't have it, how can we get enough to survive? If a modest amount is flowing through our life, how much should we save? For what? How much should we give away? To whom? We find ourselves, like it or not, devoting considerable attention to money. If we don't *serve* it as our ultimate concern, we can easily find ourselves bogged down in *servicing* it. Money's presence demands attention to balancing the checkbook, stretching the paycheck, prioritizing the bills, figuring how to save something, scouting for bargains, attending to payment deadlines.

It's Dangerous

This demanding expenditure of energy is dangerous to our spiritual health. We find ourselves fretting about it more than we should. And the very thing we fret about, if we should suddenly find ourselves with an abundance of it, poses a different kind of danger. The gospels stamp a big "hazardous material" label on money. Jesus' overriding assessment is: handle with care, if you have to handle it at all. "Take care to guard against all greed, for though one may be rich, one's life does not consist of possessions" (Luke 12:15). The rich man in Jesus' parable was condemned simply because he enjoyed his wealth without sharing it with poor Lazarus who languished at his gate (Luke 16:19–23). Jesus' advice to an idealistic young man was to give all his money away. When he couldn't do that, Jesus remarked, "It is easier for a camel to pass through the eye of a needle than for one who is rich to enter the Kingdom of God" (Matthew 19:24).

Money is a powerful magnet for our deep attention, so powerful that it can alter our fundamental orientation. "No one can serve two superiors. You will either hate one and love the other, or be attentive to one and despise the other. You cannot give yourself to God and Money" (Matthew 6:24*). Early Christians believed that "The love of money is the root of all evils" (1 Timothy 6:10).

But it didn't stop some of them from continuing to love it, and others from deferring to it. The Letter of James pointed out how money can command favorable treatment. "Suppose there should come into your assembly a person wearing gold rings and fine clothes and, at the same time, a poor person dressed in shabby clothes. Suppose further you were to take notice of the well-dressed one and say, 'Sit right here in the seat of honor; and to the poor one, 'You can stand!' or 'Sit over here by my footrest.' Haven't you in such a case discriminated in your hearts? Haven't you set yourselves up like judges who hand down corrupt decisions?" (James 2:1–4). Of course. But it's a corrupt decision that was, and still is, made frequently. People who have considerable money not only tend to get good seats in church, but are often treated with a deference elsewhere that has nothing to do with their personal character and everything to do with their bulging bank balance.

And yet we know, deep down, that wealth's seductiveness is based on an illusion. Money promises security and we all want security. But money's security is false. "Surrounded by treasure, we lie ill at ease," ancient Chinese wisdom had it. Instead of security, money delivers anxiety. Money promises power. But true power comes from character, not from cash. We look up to people who are strong personally, who have high ideals, whose personal compass points in the right direction. People who are merely rich become the butt of jokes. Money also promises happiness. Unfortunately, those who have money testify as with one voice that it doesn't deliver happiness. A Japanese proverb says, "The gods only laugh when people ask them for money."

Whenever money comes up in Jesus' ambience, a big caution light flashes. Look out, this is powerful stuff, it can cause a lot of trouble. We can't serve it and serve God at the same time. We can't be a slave to money, make it our primary concern, sacrifice love and energy and ideals to make it and make more of it and keep it and multiply it. If we do, we can't serve God at the same time. Nor can we truly love our neighbor when we're preoccupied with money. "Where your treasure is, there also will your heart be" (Matthew 6:21). If money is our treasure, we're only halfhearted about everything else.

No wonder that John Wesley, a profoundly spiritual leader, could say that when money came his way, he got rid of it fast.

WISE USE

A nonviolent response to money's danger is to be carefully restrained around it. Again, Lao Tzu: "To take all you want is never as good as to stop when you should." Gandhi was even more emphatic: "Civilization, in the real sense of the term, consists not in the multiplication, but in the deliberate and voluntary reduction of wants. This alone promotes real happiness and contentment, and increases the capacity for service...We must keep the ideal constantly in view, and in the light thereof, critically examine our possessions, and try to reduce them." A nonviolent attitude toward money calls for constant vigilance over one's desires, one's wants, constant discernment whether something is necessary or superfluous, whether we have too much when others don't have enough. Then, as Gandhi said, however much we have, try to reduce. A nonviolent approach to money calls for us constantly to be in a reduction mode rather than an acquisition mode.

The nonviolent goal for money is decency—not luxury, and also not deprivation. The nonviolent goal is the kind of life where basic necessities are available, including necessities of the spirit. Vatican II outlined these necessities:

> There must be made available to all people everything necessary for leading a life truly human, such as food, clothing and shelter; the right to choose a state of life freely and to found a family, the right to education, to employment, to a good reputation, to respect, to appropriate information, to activity in accord with the upright norm of one's own conscience, to protection of privacy and to rightful freedom in matters religious.

This catalogue of basic human needs and basic human rights spells out the components of decent living. No one anywhere in the world should be deprived of any of them. And to fulfill almost all of them takes money. The exceptions are a good reputation, and respect. Money, especially a lot of it, could actually be a hindrance to reputation and respect, which depend on the quality of one's character rather than the quantity of one's possessions. Even religious freedom demands money, to build and maintain appropriate places of worship, to travel to them, and to be freed from subsistence demands in order to engage in their activities.

If decency is the goal, a certain amount of money is necessary to achieve it. How much money varies from culture to culture, and from time to time in history. A nonviolent attitude toward money is to see that I have enough to achieve decency, and that others do, too.

A nonviolent attitude will also see how money's undeniable persuasive power can be used to help correct abuses by, for example, boycotting certain industries known to perpetrate injustice. The Nestle corporation changed its marketing of infant formula in Third World countries because of such a boycott. General Electric got out of the nuclear weapons business after a similar boycott. Agribusinesses in California began to negotiate with the United Farm Workers when conscientious people around the country refused to buy table grapes.

NONVIOLENT POVERTY
Gandhi said that poverty is the worst form of violence. He was referring to the destitution that afflicts a majority of the world's people beyond their ability to do anything about it—because of crop failures, maldistribution of food, exploitative labor practices, lack of medical care. This is the poverty that is violent. The constant teaching of the world's great religious leaders is to reach out and help, to use one's resources to alleviate that kind of poverty. And until that poverty is alleviated everywhere in the world, which it will be in the Compassionate Commonwealth, a nonviolent attitude will treat everyone equally, with respect for

their innate dignity regardless of their wealth or lack of it.

To alleviate violent poverty worldwide takes action on two levels—the systemic area of economic change, of political policies, of massive redistribution of resources. It also demands action on the personal level—reaching out to help Lazarus at the gate, the needy family next door or down the street. Both of these presuppose the presence of personal means with which to engage. Gandhian nonviolence would discourage anyone deliberately becoming so poor that one lacks these means. There may well be a certain irresponsibility in deliberately making oneself poor and expecting to be taken care of by those who have means. When a family member chooses such a course, it imposes unnecessary burdens on the other members, or on society at large which has to come to the rescue. Charming as such irresponsibility might be at a certain age, it is not compatible with the Gandhian principle of *ahimsa,* non-harm. Gospel Nonviolence presupposes economic competence, either personal or communal, if at all possible. Gospel Nonviolence or Gandhian *satyagraha* is the ability to serve, to give, to minister. It is not the condition of imposing on the resources of others. This ability is not exclusively monetary. Human strength, wit, courage, agility can all be used in helping ways.

Eileen Egan described what I would call nonviolent poverty as "having what one needs for a truly human life with the emphasis on simplicity of life so that there will something left over for those who are in need. Such a broad concept allows for many things—education and some leisure, as well as adequate clothing, food and shelter."

Jesus, Gandhi, and King all lived that way. Jesus gave up an adequate income as a carpenter in Nazareth for the role of itinerant preacher. Although he often lived off the generosity of those who offered hospitality in the tradition of the Middle East, he and his band of followers had a common purse to provide for their necessities. Their voluntary poverty stopped well short of destitution.

Gandhi started out as a lawyer, adopting the life-style of a young British barrister. He gradually divested himself of these trappings, ending up as a poor man in a loincloth with whom the poorest of the poor in India could identify. This was the secret of his success in rousing the entire nation in his nonviolent campaign for independence. Yet Gandhi lived in an ashram which provided for the needs of its members, supplemented by royalties from his writings. He lived simply, but adequately.

Martin Luther King, raised in an African American middle-class neighborhood in Atlanta, always lived modestly, but never reduced himself to the level of begging. He distributed his Nobel Peace Prize stipend among a number of civil rights organizations. Fees from speaking and writing went to the Movement, but he always made sure that his family had sufficient income for their needs.

COMPLICITY

Given the current international economic system, it's not possible for one's involvement in money to be totally nonviolent. A substantial part of tax money goes to pay for instruments of war and preparations for war. The financial institution to which we entrust our money may have investments in industries which pollute or exploit. The company that issues the credit card we use may charge exorbitant interest to those who can least afford the payments. The system does not allow a totally nonviolent use of our money. And we are necessarily embroiled in the system. What we can do, though, as in so many other areas of life, is to be on the lookout, try to avoid the worst abuses, and see, without becoming totally absorbed in the process, that our money uses are as nonviolent as we can make them.

QUESTIONS FOR REFLECTION AND DISCUSSION

1. How do *you* decide how much money you need?
2. List some of the dangers money poses in people's lives.
3. What is the relation between money and "success"?
4. How would you define a life of *decency* for yourself?
5. Why have great religious teachers advocated poverty as an important ingredient of a spiritual life? How do you react to this advice?

There is no time left for anything but to make peace work a dimension of our every waking activity.   —Elise Boulding

NONVIOLENT TIME

It's become a cliché to say that modern life is complex, that there's too much to do and not enough time to do it. Life seems to be slipping by accompanied by the inexorable ticking of our timepieces. Busyness is one of the characteristics of a culture of violence. Getting overly involved in trivia is a way of doing violence to ourselves. It traps us in constant stress and irritability and a feeling of fatigue, as well as keeping us from grappling with the climate of violence all around us. Trivia's temptation is great.

Typical time management literature details ways of becoming more efficient, of making better use of our time by employing techniques to get more done in a shorter period. All too often the result is that we find we have more to do. "Work tends to expand to fill the time allotted for it," somebody named Parkinson observed. This kind of time management is an enabler of the culture of violence. It encourages people to jump from one thing to another, to devote energy to getting more done rather than thinking through problems or working out conflicts or identifying priorities.

So many matters press in on us, there's so much to do, that there's a temptation of finding our identity in what we accomplish, of feeling that we *are* what we *do*. Our attitude toward the time we have at our disposal is a critical component of our nonviolent attitude. What we do with our time expresses our deepest beliefs about the meaning of our life. It's the way we have of showing just what is our ultimate concern.

If we would become more personally nonviolent, we need to take a hard look at all this busyness, and make some significant adjustments. We need a radically different approach. We start by coming to terms with what time itself actually is.

Our language speaks of time as something concrete. Ordinary conversations refer to time as if it were were real and rigid. We say we waste time, make time, fill time, buy time, give time, take time, manage time. We find ourselves thinking of it as something substantial, like a natural resource. "He gave me what was most valuable to him, his time." We feel we have to use it efficiently, fill it profitably.

TIME'S RELATIVITY

In fact, time itself is elusive. It's not tangible, like money. Time, in fact, doesn't even exist outside the human mind. There's no reality out there that we can point to and say, There, that's time. Clocks are not time, calendars are not time. They only indicate time, give us a measurement. Time itself is what the scholastic philosophers called an *ens rationis*, something that is found only in our thought processes. It has a foundation in reality, but time itself exists only in the mind. Time, as Aristotle defined it, is the measure of motion. Motion exists. Waves roll in, flowers bloom, the moon revolves around the earth and the earth around the sun. We walk, we talk, we think, we sleep, we build, we read, we go places, we make love. Time itself is our way of measuring the duration of these activities.

And around the world time hasn't always been measured in the same way. The day is a basic unit. For some, a day began at sunrise and ended just before the next sunrise. For others, a new day began at sunset, the end of the previous day. The Jewish Sabbath starts at sunset on Friday, because in ancient Israel a day was considered to begin at sundown, when the previous day ended. Later, in the Roman era, a day was considered to begin at dawn. The Romans determined time as so many hours after dawn. Jesus was nailed to the cross at the sixth hour after dawn, about noon in that Middle Eastern springtime when the days and nights were almost equal.

Another basic unit has been the year, marking the annual cycle of the seasons. Some cultures considered the moon as the primary determinant in the cycle, others the sun. The "new year" began when the old year ended, whenever that was considered to be. In ancient Israel the new year started in the fall, the equivalent of the sundown of the old year. The Chinese New Year occurs in the spring, after the winter-ending old year. Our designation of January 1 as New Year's Day is a matter of agreement, as is our accepting midnight as the demarcation line between days. There's nothing natural about either of these "times." They're based solely on human convention, not on anything in the world of nature.

"Standard" time, the current mode of measurement, came into existence only in the nineteenth century, with the expansion of the railroads. When trains crossed a continent, it was important to railroad companies to be able to schedule arrivals and departures according to the same measurements. Standard Time became the measure of the motion of the trains. Gradually, nations came to agree on a fixed delineation of time around the world. The globe was divided into 24 areas of about 15 degrees longitude, with Greenwich, England, the center, and areas east and west of Greenwich being so many hours ahead or behind. Various areas of the world made their own adjustments. China, extending over what would be five zones, decreed that the whole country would be on the same time as Beijing. And India advanced its time a half hour ahead of the standard measurement. The zones fluctuate in eccentric variations to accommodate political boundaries.

All of which is to say that time is arbitrary, a mental construct. What we consider to be fixed intervals is only the fairly recent result of international agreements to facilitate trade and travel.

Time's Reality

The reality behind these measurements we call time is our human activity. When we say, "There are only 24 hours in a day," or, "I wish I had more time," or "I can give you a half hour," or "We need to use our time well," we are in fact pointing to the reality of our lives, our actions, and how we decide to order them. We wake up in the morning, we live through the day, we go to sleep at night. That's what we really have to work with, ourselves and what we choose to do with our bodies and minds and spirit, the totality of our waking life. What we call "time" is no more than the hourly, daily, weekly, and yearly measurement of what we decide to do with ourselves.

And we make continual judgments about what to do in these hourly, daily, weekly, and yearly slots. Those judgments are based on what we consider more or less important, more or less urgent than other activities. We don't, in reality, "spend time" on projects or people. We do what we consider desirable or pleasurable or satisfying or necessary. And, incidentally, we measure it by how many hours or minutes on the clock or the sundial or the hourglass we devote to it. When I say, "I didn't do something because I didn't have enough time," what I really mean is, "I didn't do something because I decided to do something else instead," something I considered more important, for whatever reason. When I say I don't have enough time to do all the things I want to do, what I mean is that I haven't yet realized that I can't do everything I would like to do, I haven't prioritized the possibilities, and I haven't come to accept that the low priority items just aren't going to get done.

One advantage of the clock is that it helps us do that prioritizing. If we don't do it, we risk getting caught up in immediate demands, the result being that we neglect some activities that are really more important.

The essence of *nonviolent* time is to discern which of the many possibilities out there are more important, which are less important, and act first on the former. Stephen Covey suggests that we think of our life as guided by a compass rather than a clock. It's much more effective to point ourselves in the right direction than always to be glancing anxiously at our watch. If we get more done in a shorter time, what so often happens is that we see we have more to do—unless we have set our priorities and stick to them, unless we keep our sights on the compass rather than the clock.

QUALITY TIME

I have found it helpful to assess possible activities in four categories: urgent, vital, necessary, and, lastly, desirable for any other reason. "Urgent" are those pressing matters calling for immediate attention, demands made from the outside that substantially affect my life. Urgent matters might be an accident that needs rushing to the emergency room, or a flood in the bathroom, or a sick child, or the outbreak of a war. I must deal with emergencies at the expense of other things I would normally be doing.

Those affairs are "vital" which have high value to me; they may or may not be urgent. Reaching out to help someone in need is vital. Measures to stem the tide of violence or to help alter unjust economic systems are vital. Helping to resolve conflicts, near at hand or far away, is vital. Finding creative ways of dealing with the gangs infiltrating our neighborhood is vital. Time with loved ones is vital. So is associating with peace people. So is keeping up on what's going on in the world. As Elise Boulding said, our time is too short to do anything but what is conducive to peace. Peace work is vital for those who would follow the Nonviolent Christ.

Short of vital are all those "necessary" tasks that keep the infrastructure of life in place, like cooking, paying the bills, going to work, maintaining good physical and mental and spiritual health. We keep our mind alert and spirit lively through reading, meditating, sharing with friends, listening to people who know more than we do. All of these, in the context of the Nonviolent Christ, are forms of prayer.

When I am in adequate *physical* shape, not (too much) overweight, fairly strong, moderately flexible, I have more energy, greater staying power. Exercise helps alleviate tension. An additional bonus of regular *outdoor* exercise is a positive appreciation of the sun and wind, and the changing moods of the seasons.

The last category are those possibilities that are not urgent or vital or necessary, but are desirable for any number of reasons. Jean-Paul Sartre wrote about the "facticity" of life, the nitty-gritty physical realities that make up so much a part of our existence. These realities need attending to. In our home we say, "The chores need to be done."

THE TEMPTING TRIVIA

But the facticity of life can turn into trivia and threaten to swamp us. Tony and Robbie Fanning describe a familiar feeling.

Nothing can be more depressing than having every free minute taken by a house in constant need of repair, a lawn that needs mowing, a car that won't start, a tool you can't find to fix the car...What's depressing is not that this work is never-ending and time-consuming, but that it's never what you want to be doing at the time.

The trivia of life include watching television, or exchanging gossip, fiddling with the furniture. In this category I also place the ringing telephone. It sounds urgent, but it really isn't—unless we choose to treat it that way. When Janice and I are involved in something vital or necessary, we don't answer the phone. An answering machine screens the calls. If it turns out to be urgent or vital or necessary, then we pick up. Most calls can be returned later, at time set aside for them.

Any time we find ourselves having too much to do even after prioritizing, we can consider how much is thrust upon us by the culture of violence. Modern communications have brought more and more information into our range of acquisition. We often feel we have to act on all that extra information, or at least pay attention to it. A friend said, "I'm a news junkie," meaning that he spent a lot of time watching or listening to or reading what is called the news. The television set that lures us with seventy-five or a hundred and five channels, the magazine rack with a dozen alluring fitness publications, another dozen about automobiles, a half dozen about "news," fifteen about beauty and glamour, a whole shelf about "people"—all attempt to attract our attention. And that's just reading.

Modern methods of production have made it possible to acquire more and more "things." Modern advertising makes it more pleasurable to acquire those "things." And modern credit arrangements make it increasingly possible to purchase them. All of this results in an abundant crop of attention grabbers. The number of possibilities to fill our time is overwhelming. A few of them might even be worthwhile!

In a society with a high standard of living, where more goods and services are available, members of that society almost always feel a lack of time. The more "things" in our life, the more attention people feel compelled to give them. And since time is the measure of motion, including our attention, more things can easily mean less time. The result is a near-constant occupation or preoccupation with the "things" in our life, a condition of perpetual busyness where we're always doing something but we don't have "time" for other things we'd like to do. And this kind of busyness is socially acceptable. Stephen Covey has observed that

> Most people expect us to be busy, overworked. It's become a status symbol in our society—if we're busy, we're important; if we're not busy, we're almost embarrassed to admit it. Busyness is where we get our security. It's validating, popular, and pleasing. It's also a good excuse for not dealing with the first things in our lives.

Living in nonviolent time includes simplifying. In this culture of superabundance, we will take care not to become prisoners of our possessions. We will be ever alert to eliminate some, minimize the maintenance of others, and acquire very few new ones.

It's important, in the words of traditional wisdom, to plan the work and work the plan. I try not to let the list of what I have to do get too long. When it does, I know I have to eliminate most of the items that are not vital or necessary. Of course, this is my ideal. I usually end up doing quite a few things that are only desirable—then find myself wondering, where did the time go? Meaning, what did I do with my day? Actually, I know darned well where it went. It went to the trivia.

Nonviolent time really is a nonviolent expenditure of our energy. We say yes to what is vital and necessary, deal with what is urgent as it comes up, and decide judiciously among everything else. When the less important press on the more important, we have to have the firmness to say no. Saying no, of course, requires courage, courage to take responsibility for our actions, courage to direct them according to that compass which points in the direction of the Nonviolent Christ. It's definitely in our best interest—and in the best interest of everyone around us.

QUESTIONS FOR REFLECTION AND DISCUSSION

1. If time is nothing but the measure of motion, why does it seem so real in itself?

2. Review a typical day in your week just past. Was there much "busyness" in that day, or were all your activities essential?

3. How do you decide between essential and nonessential activities?

4. Contemporary life pressures us with having too much to do and not enough time to do it. Contemporary life also presents us with a culture of violence. Is there a connection between time-pressure and violence, or is it just coincidental that both are characteristics of contemporary life?

5. How can you make your own personal time more nonviolent?

CHAPTER FIFTEEN

In the absence of justice, what is sovereignty but organized robbery?
                                                    —St. Augustine

TELLING IT LIKE IT IS

S t. Augustine said that a nation without justice is nothing more than a large band of robbers. And, in the same vein, small bands of robbers, he said, were petty kingdoms, little nations. His description of how these petty kingdoms can grow large prefigures the history of modern nations:

> They also are groups of men, under the rule of a leader, bound together by a common agreement, dividing their loot according to a settled principle. If this band of criminals, by recruiting more criminals, acquires enough power to occupy regions, to capture cities, and to subdue whole populations, then it can with fuller right assume the title of kingdom, which in the public estimation is conferred on it, not by the renunciation of greed, but by the increase of impunity.

Augustine's description from the fifth century sounds uncomfortably like the spread of the United States in the nineteenth, when it went from the original thirteen colonies on the eastern seaboard across the Great Plains out to the west coast, confiscating the lands of native peoples, killing many who resisted, grabbing chunks of territory from Mexico, and declaring itself a single nation from sea to shining sea. "Manifest Destiny," it was called in the oratorical flourish of nineteenth-century *hubris*.

This expansion did not at all happen by what Augustine

called the renunciation of greed. Quite the opposite. Greed was encouraged in land grabs and gold rushes. The expansion became fixed not by the renunciation of greed but, as Augustine put it, by an increase in impunity—nobody was big enough or strong enough to stop it. And so a relatively small band of robbers became large and continued to become larger, extending its reach across the Pacific and northward nearly to the Pole.

But that's history, however uncomfortable the history might be. Whatever the past, we are living now, at the dawn of a new millennium, citizens of the wealthiest and most powerful country in the history of the human race, trying to see what the Nonviolent Christ would have us see, trying to live the way the Nonviolent Christ would have us live.

What we see, in this United States of America, is decidedly a mixed picture. We see "beautiful spacious skies, amber waves of grain, purple mountain majesties across a fruited plain." We see generous, hardworking, ingenious people, like the neighbors next door or our friends at church. We see a system of choosing those who govern us by elections rather than military coups, a democratic political process that has been in place for over two centuries. But we also see millions of people in poverty, corporate downsizing throwing more millions out of work or into a permanent state of employment anxiety where a person's worth is measured by the ability to consume. We see tax laws favoring the already wealthy, and welfare reform punishing the already poor. And we also see that the democratic political process is increasingly controlled by Big Money, by those who can finance the hugely expensive electoral campaigns for high office.

Our country's economic moves outside its boundaries mirror its economic policies inside. Corporations take advantage of cheap labor in Latin America and Asia. Cozy alliances with the rich and powerful in those regions keep their people poor and available. At a 1996 United Nations summit meeting on hunger, the United States, almost alone among the nations represented, insisted that there should be no international declaration of a legal right to food. Instead, it pointed to free trade as the key to ending hunger in the world. We know what happens when "free" trade becomes widespread: the rich and powerful become more rich and more powerful, the poor and dispossessed become more poor and more dispossessed. A group of church leaders in the Philippines put it this way:

> The subjection of the poor to the total free play of market forces, unrestrained by social justice and arm of a responsible government, leads only to further impoverishment and misery. Throwing less developed nations, like the Philippines, into unequal competition with advanced industrialized countries in an arena of total free trade condemns them to perpetual dependence and underdevelopment. In place of unbridled free trade, the Church calls for fair trade within a just international economic order.

Fair trade instead of free trade, they say.

But to keep it free instead of fair, internally as well as externally, our nation is armed to the teeth. Gun ownership proliferates among private citizens, fearful of the less affluent among us. An active duty armed force of a million and a half men and women, based strategically on every continent, is equipped with the most advanced weaponry that technological ingenuity can design and produce—prepared to suppress international threats to our status. The United States has three thousand nuclear warheads deployed on sophisticated missiles, ships, and aircraft, capable of destroying the whole of civilization should the order be given. And, tucked away in secret stockpiles in this country and abroad, chemical agents and deadly germs wait to be unleashed on whoever would be unfortunate enough to provoke us. Our government, whichever political party is in power, intends to use any or all of the weapons at its disposal to defend our "vital interests," however it chooses to define those interests on any given day. It relies on powerful agencies using deadly force to maintain its present position of world supremacy. It instinctively recognizes that opposition to this supremacy will arise. Hence the unquestioned support of intelligence agencies and military hardware, in a near desperate trust that these can hold the fort.

The Way It Is

Centuries ago, Augustine said that a nation grounded in violence and greed would be "characterized by war and dissension," by domestic unrest, and by the struggle to maintain power abroad. And sadly, he said, there's no end to it:

Even when it conquers, its victory can be mortally poisoned by pride, and if, instead of taking pride in the success already achieved, it takes account of the nature and normal vicissitudes of life and is afraid of future failure, then the victory is merely momentary.

When the Soviet enemy crumbled in confusion and the United States emerged as the only remaining superpower, it found a bunch of little nations snipping at its heels, and has remained perpetually armed and aggressive (Grenada, Panama, Iraq) ever since.

One government institution serves as a symbol of the whole sordid picture and projects the worst of the nation: the Central Intelligence Agency. Organized at the beginning of the Cold War in the late 1940s, the Agency was explicitly given the charge of fighting fire with fire. The Doolittle Report of that era defined the CIA's role:

It is now clear that we are facing an implacable enemy whose avowed objective is world domination by whatever means and at whatever cost...We must learn to subvert, sabotage and destroy our enemies by more clever, more sophisticated and more effective methods than those used against us.

The purpose of the CIA was not just to gather information from around the world, as its name would imply. Its purpose was also to "subvert, sabotage and destroy" our perceived enemies by any means deemed effective, including bribery, torture, and murder. These actually go by the euphemistic phrase "covert operations." Agents who gather the information include spies.

Covert operators include assassins. The CIA, essentially, is composed, as one observer put it, of "spooks and thugs."

For many Americans this sordid picture is so unpleasant that they—we—don't dwell on it. It falls into the same "unthinkable" category as the image of our nation as a large band of robbers. But the Nonviolent Christ calls us to face it, to name it, to see our place in it, and to figure out what to do about it—to think hard about this whole unthinkable morass.

FACE IT

As Israel Charny has said, "Human beings are at one and the same time generous creative creatures and deadly genociders." And so are nations, which are but collections of such human beings. Human history is, in Charny's words, "both a glorious epic of achievements and love and a dreadful blood-soaked nightmare of destruction." We rightly celebrate the U.S. epic of achievements and love, acknowledging the accomplishments in a spirit of appropriate patriotism. We also need to have nearby, for handy reference, a memory of the "dreadful blood-soaked nightmare of destruction" that is part of our past—massacres of native peoples, an economy built on the backs of slaves and forced laborers, a one-way flow of natural resources from other parts of the world, wars of territorial conquest, expanding brutality like the Second World War, exercises in corrupt cruelty like Vietnam.

As we face it, we press no moral indictment of those responsible, past and present. The Nonviolent Christ would not have us point fingers of blame at anyone except ourselves. "Let the one among you who is without sin be the first to throw a stone at her" (John 8:7). We have to assume good intentions, even on the part of the spooks and thugs. As John le Carré wrote about the 1989 invasion of Panama:

> Probably [the attackers] were fine sons and fathers, and all they meant to do was take out Noriega's *comandancia* until a couple of shells strayed off course, and a couple more followed. But good intentions in wartime do not easily com-

municate themselves to the subjects of them, self-restraint passes unnoticed, and the presence of a few fugitive enemy snipers in a poor suburb does not explain its wholesale incineration. It's not much help saying "We used minimum force" to terrified people running barefoot for their lives over blood and smashed glass, dragging suitcases and children with them on their way to nowhere.

What we can do is recognize what has happened, what is happening, look at it clearly, think through the unthinkable. This means sizing up systems of government, of international relations, of education, of the press, of radio and television, of the entertainment industry, of weapons producers—who is involved, who sets the tone, who goes along, who profits.

NAME IT

The Latin word for all this is *imperium*, meaning power, mastery, command, usually translated as "empire." The United States of America is an empire, in the classic mold of ancient Rome, nineteenth-century Britain, or the former Soviet Union. It has economic holdings around the world, and a large armed force to project military might wherever it is required. It seeks to cajole or control as many other people as possible to see things its way and do things its way.

Empires exist, have always existed, for two primary purposes: power and profit. It feels good to be in charge, to be Number One, to cause people to bend to one's will. And it ensures a steady flow of wealth from the periphery to the center. We evade the proper naming of it with phrases like "self determination" or "free trade," when what is really meant is "enforce the kind of government that will be friendly to us," or "make sure that whatever happens it will be to our economic benefit." Otherwise we will hurt you, and hurt you badly. Philip Berrigan put it straightforwardly:

The empire has its visionaries, with a goal of world domination. Nothing new about that! Such has been their aim for fifty years. But never have measures been so skillfully manipulated by a combination of secrecy, unlimited money, social confusion, and public apathy...The injustice of all this is stupefying—injustice toward the poor, to workers, and the environment. Opposition is predictable—and that's where the NSA [National Security Agency] and military come in. The swollen budgets of both—more money than they can spend—imply the desperate trust placed in them by the plutocrats.

By no means is the United States singular in its imperial ambitions. The ancient Romans controlled the Mediterranean basin for centuries, the longest running empire in history. The British in the last century had such a string of possessions that the sun never set on its empire—until a little brown man in India began an inexorable process of erosion. The French tried to keep up, gaining possession in Africa and southeast Asia. Then the stubborn Algerians and persistent Vietnamese forced them to start giving it up. The Japanese tried it in the Far East and the Germans in Europe under Hitler, but their empires lasted less than a decade and ended in a raging inferno of their cities and society. Russia under Stalin gobbled up lots of little neighbors and became for a few decades the mighty Soviet Union, only to retreat in confusion when its people finally had enough. On the horizon in the new millennium is the latest candidate for empire, the inscrutable country of China. Napoleon believed that "When China wakes, it will shake the world." We have no reason for complacency about China, no expectation that China with its 1.2 billion people and its tradition of the oldest continuous civilization in the world will prove immune to the temptation of *imperium*.

The New Testament has a vivid symbol for such empires: the Beast in the book of Revelation. "Then I saw a beast come out of the sea with ten horns and seven heads...To it the dragon gave its own power and throne, along with great authority" (Revelation 13:1–2). The beast does the work of the dragon, Satan, and uses false prophets to carry on its mission. Eventually, though, they will all be destroyed. "The Devil who had led them astray was thrown into the pool of fire and sulphur, where the beast and the false prophet were. There they will be tormented day and night forever and ever" (Revelation 20:10).

Our Place in It

We have no cause for feeling self-righteous as we scan this picture. We live in an empire, we partake of its largesse, we profit by its policies, we support it by our taxes. It's not as though we could escape it by moving somewhere else in the world. Were we to do so, we would only involve ourselves in some other society which, lacking justice itself, would be a slightly smaller band of robbers. And wherever in the world we moved, we would still be under some influence of the United States.

No, the truth calls for us to acknowledge our complicity. We are part of the system. We have to live with it. We can diminish the degree of our complicity by refusing to be involved in the military, by seeking employment in activities that do not exploit so greatly, by attending to the way our money is used so that it helps the victims of the empire more than its perpetrators, and especially by attempting to live in a way different than that desired by Empire. As Daniel Berrigan put it:

> A different social compact, implying a far different humanism, has been proposed by Jesus. "Serve one another." In effect: "This is the way that best responds both to your nature and to the will of God." Moreover, and of equal import, this is the "way" that most sharply sets you off from the brutalities of secular power.

Facing it, naming it, acknowledging our place in it, and trying to live in a way different from it—we are called to all of this by the Nonviolent Christ.

Questions for Reflection and Discussion

1. In what way is it accurate to compare the United States to a large band of robbers?

2. In what way is such a comparison misleading?

3. The United States has more military power than any nation on earth. What rationales are given for such power? Are they convincing?

4. What is your image of the CIA? If you were elected President of the United States, what would you do about the CIA? Could you get away with it?

5. What directional changes does the United States have to make to avoid the fate of the Beast in the book of Revelation?

The good we secure for ourselves is precarious and uncertain until it is secured for all of us and incorporated into our common life.   —Jane Addams

POLITICAL AWARENESS

We cannot *not* be involved in politics. There's no such thing as being apolitical. Not to decide is to decide. To refuse to take part in the affairs of our community is, in effect, to allow them to go on as before. Noninvolvement is a vote for the status quo. The root of "political" is the Greek word *polites,* meaning citizen, one who exists in a condition of community with others. No matter how isolated some strive to be, we are all citizens in the sense that our lives affect—and are affected by—others. Even to attempt to withdraw is a political action, an action of removing oneself from relationships. We all have responsibility for our relationships with others. In that sense the personal is political. What we do, or don't do, affects others in some way, ripples out into the broader arena.

"Political" also has to do with governing, with establishing the procedures for human beings living with each other, with maintaining, refining, and changing those procedures if necessary. They will never be perfect until the fullness of the Compassionate Commonwealth. Until then, they are more or less imperfect, sometimes very much so, as in the present empire. But they're all we've got at this time. Our responsibility as followers of the Nonviolent Christ is to try to make them somewhat better than they are. And when we embark on that effort in the spirit of the Nonviolent Christ we are, as Gandhi said, "spiritualizing the political."

Gandhian nonviolence has the negative aspect of *ahimsa,* avoiding harm as much as possible, and the positive aspect of *satyagraha,* the search for truth, the power of truth, the reaching out to help and to heal. As we ponder the political scene and decide whom to vote for, what to support, what to oppose, what issues to become involved in, how far to go, we have a guide from Gandhi:

> I will give you a talisman. Whenever you are in doubt or when the self becomes too much with you, apply the following test. Recall the face of the poorest and weakest person whom you may have seen, and ask yourself if the step you contemplate is going to be of any use over that person's life and destiny. In other words, will it lead to self-reliance for the hungry and spiritually starving millions. Then you find your doubt and your self melting away.

Jesus said, "I was hungry and you gave me food, I was thirsty and you gave me drink, a stranger and you welcomed me, naked and you clothed me, ill and you cared for me, in prison and you visited me" (Matthew 25:35–36). Today he would say, "I was homeless and you found shelter for me. I had AIDS and you made sure I was taken care of. I was sexually abused and you saw that I got help." When we decide which government policies at any level—local, state, national—to support or oppose, the first question is how they will affect those who most need help—not just in our own society but elsewhere in the world as well.

GLOBALIZATION

Interconnectedness has always been a fact. But in the past it was recognized dimly if at all except by visionaries like the Buddha, or Socrates. Jesus certainly spoke about it when he encouraged us to love our neighbor without exception. In our times the revolution in communications and transportation and, yes, weaponry, has magnified global interconnectedness into an inescapable fact of life. Globalization has already happened—in business, in ecological awareness, in personal mobility, in military power. It has also happened in many other areas—AIDS, global warming, destruction of the rain forests, the population explosion, political instability of the poorer nations, the flood of refugees, pollution of air and water. No single country can cope with these problems by itself, even when affected by them. Our political involvement needs to be sensitive to what affects people in other parts of the world as well as our own.

Trends toward human rights, social justice—small movements, partial processes—do exist. Movements that lead to a more equitable distribution of wealth need our support. Policies that make life's necessities of food, clothing, shelter, and health care available to all and at reasonable cost, need support. Programs that provide for those who are ill, or incapacitated, or too young, or mentally disabled, or temporarily unemployed, need support. Increasing the number of jobs and access to them, increasing the wages for those jobs—these need support.

The Nonviolent Christ would have us always ask: what policies and processes are being proposed that will assist those who most need help?

THE SACRED COW

The public case against increased social spending in the interest of balancing the budget or avoiding tax increases always overlooks the single largest item in the federal budget, the huge amount spent on "defense." This is the sacred cow, the golden calf, the ultimate untouchable. Ruth Leger Sivard pointed out that the cost of one Trident II submarine-launched ballistic missile equals the cost of Vitamin A supplements for 100,000,000 children for one year. The cost of one Abrams M-1 tank equals 530,000 vials of insulin essential to diabetes. The cost of one Tomahawk cruise missile equals 1,200 wells equipped with hand pumps for families without water resources.

Buying fewer tanks or missiles would release enough money to provide vitamins to prevent disease, and insulin to treat diabetics, for hundreds of thousands of children. Why, then, keep on producing and paying for so many tanks and missiles and other military machinery? Why prostrate before the golden calf? One answer is "jobs." Another is "careers." The *Defense Monitor* described whose careers are involved in ensuring an endless supply of external threats:

> The members of this broad security establishment are quite varied. They can be found among military retirees, corporate executives, foreign service officers and retirees, academics, analysts in think tanks and the CIA, editors, reporters, columnists, commentators, television pundits, publishers, and congressional staffers...These people share and promote a common theme: America must lead the world, particularly where military force is required. The concept of U.S. interests they impose upon the public is largely unrelated to the well-being of most American citizens...Sincere or not, many members of the security establishment worry that they would soon see their careers vanish if military spending is cut. They would also lose their sense of important purpose and prestige.

No conspiracy exists here. The system works this way because the people involved in the system have a personal stake in keeping it going. But for the vast majority who blindly support such expenditures, neither jobs nor careers are at stake. What is at stake is a need for enemies beyond rational geopolitical realities. Too many Americans see the world as dangerous and filled with peril. Perhaps, deep down, we sense that we have so much more than most, and fear that, out of envy or righteous anger, they will rise up and try to equalize the economics. As a high ranking military officer, now retired, put it:

> Without enemies how could we justify spending more than $250 billion every year on a worldwide military empire? Only if the world is perceived as "dangerous" will taxpayers willingly pay this enormous bill.

Let's put a billion dollars in perspective. If one earned $1,000 a *day*, it would take a total of 2,740 *years* to earn a billion dollars. What's at stake in the need for enemies? When we keep the focus on external opponents, we keep it away from internal indecencies. It's widespread, it may not even be conscious, but leaders all over the world know, as though learned in some universal primer of politics, that they can rely on the support of their people when the people believe there is a serious threat to their way of life, that there are enemies out there.

Justice and Charity

The American empire does incorporate a certain degree of internal justice. We have a constitution and a system of laws which, on paper, apply equally to all even when the people administering the system favor the wealthy and powerful. Progress has been made in correcting some past abuses, like guaranteeing a minimum wage for those who have a job (even though that minimum wage keeps a family below the poverty line). We have preserved the rights of labor to organize. Procedures are in place to give some financial help to those who are elderly or disabled. We have yet to see the achieving of full justice, defined as a condition where all people have access to the goods and services of the community so that no one is hungry, deprived, or exploited.

While the empire does not achieve full justice, it does extol charity. It rewards philanthropy with tax breaks and public adulation. Those responsible for maintaining the empire sense that in some deep way handouts to the poor, considered "charity," maintain rather than disrupt the status quo. Reverend Alison Boden, Dean of Chapel at the University of Chicago, has given a lucid explanation of this connection. She was preaching on the story of a woman anointing Jesus' feet at a dinner party. Judas protested that the costly ointment could instead be sold and the money given to the poor. Jesus told him, "Leave her alone. Let her keep this for the day of my burial. You always have the poor with you, but you do not always have me" (John 12:8). Dean Boden said:

I read these words not as an excuse but as an explanation

by Christ: as long as...people of faith and good will make their peace with injustice and soothe their conscience with charity, then we will always have the poor with us... Charity is giving; justice is sharing. Charity is kindness; justice is righteousness. Charity is donating what is surplus—time, items, articles, money, or three hundred denarii to spend on perfume. Justice is partitioning what is essential—education, health, homes and food. Charity is comfortable, it warms the heart. Charity does good. Justice makes right...All the charity in the world will not fundamentally affect the lot of the countless children, women and men who are desperately poor, because it doesn't begin to touch the power imbalance that holds them there. Justice does. I hear Jesus telling Judas, as long as you continue to tell yourself that charity is enough, you will always have the poor with you.

This is not to downgrade the value of giving as an exercise of selflessness. As Ched Myers said, "Making regular donations to a social agency, volunteering at a soup kitchen, or sponsoring a child in the Third World should be valued as nothing more or less than expressions of basic human kindness." They are acts of generosity, signs of caring.

There is a place for charity in our society. It is good to give and to reach out to others. But for many, charity is preferable to justice because it requires no fundamental change in the status quo. Andrew Carnegie believed that the wealthy had an obligation to return money to charity. "And besides," he said, "it provides a refuge from self-questioning." Until any society reaches a high level of justice, such expressions of charity are vitally necessary. But they don't, they won't, they can't, solve the problem. As long as this kind of charity is seen as even a partial answer, "you will always have the poor with you," as Jesus said.

BEYOND LABELS

Those who advocate severely slashed "defense" spending in the interest of helping people who are poor and dispossessed should not be deterred by being called utopian, or socialist, or the lately fashionable label of opprobrium, liberal. We're beyond labels. We're looking at reality. Serious regard for the material and spiritual well-being of every member of the human family is a hallmark of Gospel Nonviolence. When we see movement in that direction, we're for it, even when the movement is called utopian or socialist or liberal. When someone accuses me of "simply buying the liberal agenda," I have to think why the label, why not the substance?

Another unfashionable label in the City of This World is "multiculturalism." The fact is that because of the increasingly greater mobility of our times, we live and work and interact with people from different ethnic and cultural backgrounds. Gospel Nonviolence, with its reverence for what is good in everyone and its emphasis on searching for truth, helps us see the value in getting to know and respect people from a variety of cultures, to stretch beyond the limitations of our own traditions. Albert Nolan has said:

> Real solidarity begins when we recognize together the advantages and disadvantages of our different social backgrounds and present realities and the quite different roles that we shall therefore have to play while we commit ourselves together to the struggle against oppression.

The City of This World values cultural superiority over real solidarity. The preferred mode of dealing with those who are different from the dominant culture is some form of segregation, keeping them apart. When segregation is exposed in its crudity, the dominant culture then turns to assimilation—let them become like us—which is the other side of the coin of segregation.

NO ANSWER YET
We have to be careful. A certain amount of socially beneficent largesse is necessary to keep a capitalistic economic system from siege by those it hurts. And it does hurt many. Capitalism is

based on the production of goods for profit, not necessarily for meeting human needs. It relies on competition to keep prices down so that goods can be sold. The profit motive plays to greed. Competition plays to heartlessness. And the whole system demands a certain level of unemployment in order to keep wages within what are considered acceptable bounds. Because unemployment is the road to poverty, a capitalistic economy needs certain "benefits" in place to keep the unemployed from becoming a sullen, threatening mass.

To think that if abuses can be corrected the system will work well for everyone is to miss the point. There's no such thing as compassionate capitalism. Compassionate capitalists there may be, who give generously to "the poor." But the system itself generates the poor. Abuses are not peripheral, the capitalistic economic system itself is an abuse. If all we do is support the current "liberal agenda," we are really putting band-aids on cancer. But band-aids are better than nothing. Better a little help than increasing the misery. The big answer is not yet in. For a follower of the Nonviolent Christ, armed revolution cannot be the answer. *Nonviolent* revolution, yes, but toward what?

I'm haunted by a remark made by a Swedish woman at a conference in Switzerland a few years ago. "It's hard to be poor in Sweden," she said. "You really have to work at it." Programs were in place in Sweden to help those who needed help. Social workers sought them out to make sure they got it. Swedes received 90% of their previous income if they were sick, injured, or stayed home to take care of sick children. Should Swedish-style socialism characterize the Compassionate Commonwealth? Or some widespread system of cooperatives? I confess I don't know. The *National Catholic Reporter* editorialized that current Catholic teaching "did not offer insights or directions into reversing a national and global economic system that primarily benefits the rich." We know the problem. As the new millennium dawns, we're not too sure about the answer, except that we know somehow it will involve communities of caring, concerned people striving to work together.

VOTING PLUS

I believe in always voting, going through the motions of casting a ballot. But I know that, except for local candidates, my vote means little. The two-party system seldom offers a real choice of alternatives. Both parties are in complete service of the empire. William Sloan Coffin has said that we have in effect a one-party system in this country, a National Party. It has two caucuses, Democratic and Republican, and they occasionally switch off in holding the office of President.

Our political involvement will be much more widespread than voting. Political responsibility includes communicating with officials about pertinent pieces of legislation, attempting to influence public opinion by letters to the editor and private conversations, taking public stands on vital issues. It does not include making contributions to national candidates, because these are amply supported by Big Money intent on preserving the ways of empire.

Because our goal of the Compassionate Commonwealth transcends national boundaries, our political responsibility extends to helping move toward a social order that reflects the unity of the human family.

QUESTIONS FOR REFLECTION AND DISCUSSION

1. What is your feeling about getting involved in politics?
2. How does economic globalization affect your own life?
3. Why is there such resistance to cutting the defense budget?
4. Why is there such resistance to spending more tax money on human needs?
5. How do you see yourself involved in both justice and charity?

CHAPTER SEVENTEEN

Keep your eyes on the prize, hold on, hold on.

—A Traditional Spiritual

TOGETHER WE CAN

The Nonviolent Christ helps us keep our eyes on the prize, the City of God, which we have undertaken to build. We don't have to do it alone. Today, as over the past 2,000 years, millions have been inspired to undertake building some part of that City, feeling called as did the women and men who answered Jesus' first call in biblical Palestine. Simon Peter and his brother Andrew left their trade of fishing when Jesus walked by on the shore and invited them to join him in another kind of fishing, ministry to humanity (Mark 1:16–18). A Samaritan woman, after a chance encounter with Jesus at a well, received the incredible news that he was the promised Messiah. She left her water jar and went back to town to tell everybody about him (John 4:28). Mary Magdalene, who with several other women had been first to the tomb after his crucifixion, did as she was asked by her risen Friend and announced the good news to all the sisters and brothers (John 20:17–18). The men, and also the women (Luke 8:1–3), who accompanied him as he was proclaiming the Kingdom were the first wave of construction workers on the City of God.

Millions more continue the effort today. Not only can we not build the City of God, the Compassionate Commonwealth, alone, we can't even acquire by ourselves the fundamental skill necessary to build it. If the City is to be constructed by service stemming from love of neighbor and enemy, we know that the basic skill for that love is self-respect, self-esteem, the proper appreciation of self. The self-love that is at the heart of love of neighbor and enemy, and therefore the foundational skill for building the City of God, absolutely needs others. The ability to affirm ourselves comes not from ourselves, but from affirmation by others whom we respect. What has been widely touted as the imperative of community is in fact vital for following the Nonviolent Christ. Community does not necessarily mean physically living together, but it does mean finding others with whom we can share our deepest values, and staying in touch with them. What we can't do alone, we can do together. It takes a village, a community effort, to raise a child. It also takes a village, a community effort, to develop the Compassionate Commonwealth.

THE CONSTRUCTION CREW

We've come a long way from enthusiastically hailing the Secular City, Harvey Cox's helpful image from the 1960s, as a symbol of God's reign. That Secular City rightly attracted our attention to the this-worldly component of the Kingdom of Heaven. But now we see clearly that we cannot identify this Kingdom with any existing political structure. Today's Secular City looks more like Augustine's City of This World. Today's Secular City sprouted a lot of weeds along with the wheat. We know that the construction crew of the City of God will be made up of those who have more of the wheat than the weeds in them. A Memphis rabbi put it this way:

> The two kinds of people who exist in this world [at any one time] are the decent and the indecent. Color, religion and nationality are irrelevant. Kindness, decency and behavior are what matter most. Our collective challenge, it seems, is to create a city and community where decent people of all races, ethnicities and religions can look into the faces of other decent people and see only one thing—God's image smiling back.

Our companions on the construction crew of the City of God

will not be restricted to any one faith or religious system. The Nonviolent Christ is, in Matthew Fox's term, "postdenominational." The Nonviolent Christ transcends denominational differences, allows us to feel communion with those of any faith tradition who are attempting to develop the Compassionate Commonwealth. Fox explained:

> Postdenominationism is about pluralism and ecumenism in religion. It is about stretching our piecemeal religious boundaries and *setting aside our boxes* to the extent that they are neither challenging us nor nourishing us deeply anymore, or to the extent that they are interfering with the pressing earth issues of our time. Denominationalism mirrors the physics of the modern era, when we were taught a parts mentality and that atoms are rugged individualists that never interpenetrate. In the name of denominationalism we have, over the centuries, fought wars, tortured people and whole towns, excommunicated one another, hated one another, competed against one another, banished one another to hell for eternity, and more or less managed to miss the point of what Jesus of Nazareth was teaching: such behavior characteristics as compassion, justice making, loving your enemies, telling the truth...It is hoped that a postdenominational era will improve our efforts to live out the message of Jesus.

GETTING ALONG

Nonviolence works because people tend to respond positively when they are treated politely, with consideration and genuine care. If we expect decency from others, we will more often than not find it. Looking around with peace eyes we see many more instances of cooperation than of hostility. Acts of violence, individual and collective, are so featured in the news media that we may mistake this "news" for the total picture of what's happening.

True, there is much violence in our culture. But there is much more decent, humane behavior. There are many more random acts of senseless kindness than random acts of senseless violence. Cooperation is people's preferred way of acting. Almost everyone wants to get along, to be helpful. Most people would rather not fight. The desire to cooperate is so common that Gandhi could call it a "law" of our species. Normal behavior is the woman who sweeps the common porch outside an apartment, the family that adopts children from a war-torn area, the neighbor who knows everyone on the block and watches out for trouble, the man who brings over a meal for a family with someone in the hospital, the pleasant stranger who greets everyone with a smiling "hello."

The story of the human race is characterized by efforts to get along much more than by violent disputes, although it's the latter that make the history books. Violence is actually exceptional. The human race has survived because of cooperation, not aggression. The Nonviolent Christ helps us take a more balanced view of the human condition than that presented in the culture of violence. Human beings are not fundamentally aggressive and in conflict, although we possess the ability to be so. The world need not necessarily be a threatening, competitive, hostile environment, although it possesses the ability to be so—and all too often is. It is more a place of opportunity for growth. We humans try to work things out most of the time with people with whom we disagree. We sidestep their unpleasantness, and direct our efforts to healing hurts rather than inflicting more of them. Personal nonviolence helps us initiate that harmony when others might be uncertain or leaning in another direction.

THE OPPOSITION

Violent behavior is learned, not instinctual. "You've got to be carefully taught," as the Rodgers and Hammerstein song put it. Unfortunately, it's learned very well in contemporary culture because it's taught very well. As Roger Rosenblatt expressed it:

> It is competitiveness that fuels capitalism. We live in a
> nation of organized rivalries; the system is designed to hurl
> young people at one another in some perpetual, semi-

mythological battle royal. To the one left standing goes the corner office.

Donald Cabana, a former executioner for the state of Mississippi, turned his life in a new direction and became an outspoken opponent of capital punishment. He said that after he stepped over the line he found it very lonely at first. Most of his former friends and colleagues quickly faded away after he renounced his previous occupation. He gained strength and courage as he began identifying coworkers for the Compassionate Commonwealth.

Those who belong to the City of This World, which Ched Myers calls "the dominant culture," have aims and ambitions considerably different from those taught by the Nonviolent Christ:

> From the moment European flags were first planted in American soil to the Gulf War in defense of U.S. oil interests, the dominant culture has proceeded on the firm conviction that we are entitled to the earth and its wealth, by any means necessary.

The Nonviolent Christ helps us make and stick with a fundamental decision as we attempt to create a global Compassionate Commonwealth that will encompass all our sisters and brothers. The decision was articulated by Albert Camus a half century ago:

> All I ask is that, in the midst of a murderous world, we agree to reflect on murder and to make a choice. After that, we can distinguish those who accept the consequences of being murderers ourselves or the accomplices of murderers, and those who refuse to do so with all their force and being.

With the Nonviolent Christ we reject being murderers and accomplices of murderers with all our force and being. But in the City of This World, unfortunately, most haven't made that decision. Those involved in murder, whether they see themselves that way or not, will not appreciate those who resist murderous systems with all their force and being. We do well not to underestimate the threat posed by the City of This World. Those whose tilt is toward, in Augustine's words, "the love of self to the exclusion of God," toward "violence and the lust for domination," often have little patience with those attempting to build the Compassionate Commonwealth. When service in charity disturbs the powers of the City of This World, the dominant culture, we can expect opposition from those powers. As Leonardo Boff put it, "Those with power...fashion crosses for those who fight for a world that is less divided between rich and poor."

The dramatic vision of the Woman and the Dragon at the heart of the book of Revelation gives a vivid image of the threat posed by this dominant culture.

> A great sign appeared in heaven: a woman clothed with the sun, with the moon under her feet...She was pregnant and in labor, crying out in pain as she was about to give birth. Then another sign appeared in heaven: a huge red dragon, with seven heads and ten horns...The dragon stood before the woman about to deliver, to devour her child the moment she gave birth...The serpent vomited a river of water from its mouth to sweep the woman away in the current. But the earth came to the woman's rescue by opening its mouth and swallowing the river that the dragon had vomited up. Then the dragon was enraged with the woman, and went off to wage war with the rest of her offspring—those who keep God's commandments and hold to the testimony of Jesus (Revelation 12:1–3,4b,15–17*).

Commitment to the Nonviolent Christ involves struggle and danger. Gil Bailie put it this way:

> The Gospel is the driving force in human history. The gates of hell shall not prevail against it. But that doesn't mean that the gates of hell won't make a ferocious effort.

But we have from the same book of Revelation the assurance of ultimate victory for those who have been faithful to the Nonviolent Christ.

The One who sat on the throne said, "Look! I'm making everything new!" and added, "Write this, for what I am saying is trustworthy and true." And the One continued, "It is finished. I am the Alpha and the Omega, the Beginning and the End. To those who are thirsty I will give drink freely from the spring of the water of life. This is the rightful inheritance of the overcomers. I will be their God and they will be my daughters and sons" (Revelation 21:5–7*).

The dream of the City of God is definitely not an impossible one.

When we act in postdenominational concert with others in a spirit of nonviolence, we are capable of achieving extraordinary results. It holds out the promise of progress as we keep our eyes on the prize of the Compassionate Commonwealth. It's the prize on which we keep our eyes and hold on, hold on, even for dear life.

QUESTIONS FOR REFLECTION AND DISCUSSION
1. Do you agree that the construction crew of the Compassionate Commonwealth must be "postdenominational"?

2. How can you identify "postdenominational" people?

3. Although cooperation is vital, competition can have some role in building the City of God. Can you imagine such a thing as "nonviolent competition"?

4. Our enthusiasm for constructing the Compassionate Commonwealth is sure to run into opposition. Why? What can we do about the opposition?

5. Have you faced times in the past year when it was very difficult to keep your eyes on the prize of the Kingdom of Heaven? Are the prospects any better for next year?

CHAPTER EIGHTEEN

This is my quest, to follow that star;
No matter how hopeless, no matter how far.
—Man of La Mancha

THE FUTURE IS NOW

In the spirit of the Nonviolent Christ we address the most crucial issues of our time. The power and presence of violence in all its forms remains the most corrosive, the most immediately threatening element in our social environment. The most pressing need is still to turn back this tide of violence, to stem the devices of exploitation, to thwart the aims of empire, to tame the desire for domination, and to relate in a better, more healthy way to others and to our environment. The Nonviolent Christ is a sound spiritual guide as we move into the twenty-first century, offering a dynamic way of dealing with the threats and frustrations with which we are faced. Confronting a culture of violence includes developing social policies to care for the neediest and most helpless among us, concern for all life, including the unborn, and devising a new relationship to our physical environment. It is renewed commitment to the responsibility of building the City of God, the Compassionate Commonwealth.

Standard mental health advice says, "Don't fret about the past and don't worry about the future. Live the present moment." Deepak Chopra put it: "The past is history, the future is mystery, the present is gift." Chopra is right about the past. It's over, it's history. We can't do anything about it except to learn from it so we don't repeat its mistakes. But the present, with which we've been gifted, is a constant exchange between daily struggle and our larger vision. And the future is not a total mystery. We have some influence on it depending on what we do in the present. Our larger nonviolent vision is the City of God, the Compassionate Commonwealth. We can help bring this vision to reality not by worrying about it, not by solving what mystery it contains, but by *living* our vision *now,* by making that future *present.*

We can choose to craft our present so that it is on the side of creation rather than the side of destruction. If we make no conscious choice about creation or destruction, then we drift with the currents of the culture. And we know those are currents of violence, currents of insensitivity, currents of power and death. Every choice we make—what we buy, what work we do, where we live, the people with whom we associate—is made in the midst of the culture of violence. Our choices will either perpetuate that culture, or help shape it in a different direction.

Gandhi taught us the inextricable intertwining of end and means. The way to bring about the end we want has to be the same as that end. You can't get peace by going to war. As A.J. Muste said, "There is no way to peace, peace is the way." We counter a culture of violence by creating a culture of nonviolence. We live according to the future we most like to see. Our future really is in our hands now, as we live it in the present.

If the Compassionate Commonwealth is characterized by justice, then we act justly now. If it is characterized by peace, then we try to live a peace-filled life now. We give up any tendency to impose our truth on others. We seek only to *offer* it to others by means of acting it out. At times this may mean a clear word in a confused meeting, or silence when everyone else is shouting, or putting our bodies in the way of the machinery of death, or stepping across the fault line in a faith-filled witness.

Because the City of God is characterized by concern for those in need, we exercise that concern for needy ones who touch our lives now. The Nonviolent Christ directs us away from a self-centered concentration on the exclusive pursuit of personal happiness and toward a greater sensitivity to others, reaching out to improve things for *them.* The Sermon on the Mount instructs us to "Stop worrying, then, over questions such as 'What are we to

eat,' or 'what are we to drink,' or 'what are we to wear?' Those
without faith are always running after these things. Seek first
God's reign, and God's justice, and all these things will be given
to you besides" (Matthew 6:31-33*). God's reign and God's justice—the Compassionate Commonwealth—is the larger vision
that guides us through the daily pressures. As we live by that
vision, we find lots of lesser things falling into place. The pressing concerns of the facticity of life don't concern us as much;
they become much less pressing.

Martin Luther King suggested that

> The first question which the priest and the Levite asked
> [on the Jericho Road] was: "If I stop to help this man, what
> will happen to me?" But...the good Samaritan reversed the
> question: "If I do not stop to help this man, what will hap-
> pen to him?"

As Dorothy Day has said, "An act of love, a voluntary taking
on oneself of some of the pain of the world, increases the
courage and love and hope of all." And Daniel Berrigan pointed
out:

> The Sermon on the Mount concerns us here and now, or
> concerns us never. In whatever modest and clumsy a way,
> we are called to honor the preference of Christ for suffer-
> ing rather than inflicting suffering, for dying rather than
> killing.... The time to obey is now.

Our nonviolent stance, practically speaking, is a way of looking at the world, at the universe around us, and saying no to the
distress and ugliness, no to the exploitation and violence. But it
is also saying yes to all that can heal the distress, transform the
ugliness, and remove the exploitation.

A NEW COSMOLOGY
The nonviolent vision expands to encompass all creation,
including the part of it we eat. We are all elements of the same

magnificent whole. For countless millennia the universe has been expanding, evolving. No longer is it appropriate to say that human beings are masters of creation and can do with it what we will. The Nonviolent Christ helps us appreciate the wisdom in what Thomas Berry calls "the New Cosmology." This comprehensive view of the totality of the universe sees the role of humans as its conscious component. Michael Dowd describes our place in the cosmos:

> We [humans] are the latest evolutionary development of an unbroken process of divine creativity that began in a stupendous explosion of light and energy. Creation was not something that happened once upon a time and then stopped; it is something that is still happening.

Because we are the self-conscious and spiritually aware ingredients of this evolving system, we have a special role to play in it. We can, as followers of the Nonviolent Christ, lead creation forward into an era where overall violence is diminished, although this will be slow, even imperceptible. Michael Dowd continues:

> Since we humans have been given the gift of awareness and the responsibility of free choice, we co-creatively participate in the evolving creation of God as we give birth to truth, beauty, justice, and love.

We help give birth, in other words, to the Compassionate Commonwealth.

The New Cosmology brings a helpful correction to human *hubris,* the assumption that humans are "in charge" of the world and can do anything we want with it. The ecological crisis, pollution of the oceans, depletion of the ozone layer, chemical agriculture, acid rain, all point to harm being done to the air we breathe and the water we drink. The apocalyptic existence of nuclear waste from power plants and weapons production with its "half-life" that assures its poisonous existence for tens of thousands of years—eternal, for all practical purposes—is a millstone around the necks of future generations. An engineering colleague of mine once said, with unbridled confidence, that the answer to nuclear waste was to put it on rockets and shoot it into the sun! The new cosmology introduces a healthy humility into our economic and industrial thinking.

And yet, a word of caution. Concentration on the Earth and its creatures, spending energy on the grass and the sea and the birds of the air, while necessary and valuable, can become so absorbing that it distracts from the nitty-gritty work of building the Compassionate Commonwealth. Violence against the Earth is sad, but violence against people is tragic. It is more difficult, but also more urgent, to explore and adopt a nonviolent way of life in the face of empires and genocides, a way that includes loving Earth and all its creatures, but concentrates on the most difficult creatures of all, we its people.

GENTLE WITNESS
This new cosmology helps us see that we don't have all the answers. Dowd again:

> The new cosmology is forcing us to make a number of significant shifts in our thinking. One of the most important of these is the shift from thinking that we could know the whole truth about something to an understanding that *everything* is evolving. It takes humility to accept the fact that truth, like everything else, is in process, and that time tends to unfold broader and deeper meanings of whatever is understood to be true.

So Gandhi could say that his life was "an experiment in truth." And, he said, "We are constantly being astonished these days at the amazing discoveries in the field of violence. But I maintain that far more undreamt of and seemingly impossible discoveries will be made in the field of non-violence."

The future to be, the nonviolent future we are trying to live now, contains much mystery. We claim but to see the direction we would like it to go: toward the Kingdom of Heaven, the Compassionate Commonwealth. We also claim to have a glimpse of how to get there, through patient, persevering, active nonviolence. If we say we'll wait until things quiet down a bit, tread water until some of this violence subsides, we're in for a long wait. But when we take the initiative, even without a large organization or expectation of great improvement, we can begin to make good things happen. King said, "The ultimate measure of a person is not where one stands in moments of comfort and convenience, but where one stands in times of challenge and controversy." Ours are times of challenge and controversy. Our attitude is not wringing of hands, not pious plaints about troubles, not wistful "if onlys." We get on with building the City of God.

Matthew's Gospel ends with Jesus giving one last instruction to his followers: "Go, therefore, and make disciples of all nations" (Matthew 28:19). As Jim Douglass explains, this means that they (we)

> transform the nations of the world by teaching them to turn from the logic of violence to the logic of love and forgiveness. That is the nature of the new age begun by Jesus' resurrection, a resurrection of all peoples and nations in a forgiving, nonviolent humanity.

We have to have the determination to go ahead, to continue hoping beyond hope. It involves the depths of our personality, what Charny calls "the ever-present, purposeful, pulsating energy or strength for being which charges the very spirit." Thanks to the Nonviolent Christ, we have this reorientation of our life force, we have made the change in the way we comport ourselves in relation to the world around us.

Gandhi said that when the practice of nonviolence becomes universal, God will reign on earth as God does in heaven. In other words, if everyone were to practice Gospel Nonviolence, whether they call it that or not, we would reach the fulfillment of the Kingdom of Heaven.

Because the Nonviolent Christ is countercultural, we will at times be seen by others to be foolish, to be "unrealistic," to be tilting at windmills when we live in his spirit. But the Nonviolent Christ calls us forward in hope—forward toward the New Jerusalem, the City of God, the Compassionate Commonwealth, the Kingdom of Heaven. By the world's standards it's an impossible dream. But by faith we know it's not so impossible, and so we carry on.

The Nonviolent Christ said, "I am with you always, until the end of the age" (Matthew 28:28). In his Spirit, we can influence and direct the course of history toward the Compassionate Commonwealth. That, and nothing less, is our goal.

QUESTIONS FOR REFLECTION AND DISCUSSION

1. The Compassionate Commonwealth is both future and present. What are some ways in which we can live the *presence* of it?

2. How can the New Cosmology (pp. 142-144) help us adjust our energies for the Compassionate Commonwealth?

3. What practical implications does Gandhi's image of an "experiment in truth" have in our walking with the Nonviolent Christ?

4. This book suggests that the way of the Nonviolent Christ is in "our best interest." Whose best interest? What interest?

5. What do we do when the dream really does seem impossible?

NOTES

PART ONE: THE NONVIOLENT CHRIST

Page

1   The epigraph at the beginning of Part One is quoted in *Gandhi on Non-Violence: A Selection from the Writings of Mahatma Gandhi*, edited and with an introduction by Thomas Merton (New York: A New Directions Paperbook, 1965), p. 40.

CHAPTER ONE. ULTIMATE CONCERN

2   Paul Tillich's discussion of faith as Ultimate Concern is contained in his book *The Dynamics of Faith* (New York: Harper & Row, Harper Torchbook, 1957), especially Part I, "What Faith Is."

4   The identification of Jesus as "an outstanding Galilean charismatic *hasid*" was made by Geza Vermes, Professor Emeritus of Jewish Studies, University of Oxford, in the newsletter *Explorations,* published by the American Interfaith Institute and the World Alliance of Interfaith Organizations (321 Chestnut Street, Philadelphia, PA 19106), Volume 10, Number 2, 1996, p. 7.

6   The quote from Lao Tzu is a variant of the translation given from Poem 56 of the *Tao Te Ching* by R.B. Blakney in *The Way of Life: Lao Tzu* (New York: Mentor Books, 1955), p. 109. Blakney's translation: "Those who know do not talk, And talkers do not know."

7   James Redfield, author of *The Celestine Prophecy*, made this observation in an interview with journalist Cecile S. Holmes of the Houston *Chronicle.* Her story, "Redfield books connect with spiritual hunger" was reprinted in the Memphis *Commercial Appeal*, Sept. 10, 1996, p. C2.

7   Dr. King used the image of the arc of the moral universe on a number of occasions, e.g., in his last SCLC Presidential Address, contained in *A Testament of Hope: the Essential Writings and Speeches of Martin Luther King, Jr.,* edited by James M. Washington (New York: Harper Collins paperback edition, 1986), pp. 245-252. The quote appears near the end of his address, on p. 252.

8   Thomas Aquinas' analysis of the virtue of humility is contained in his *Summa Theologica*, Part II-II, ques. 161, art. 2.

8   The Daniel Berrigan quote is from his article "Dear Seminarians," in *The Critic*, Vol. 41 (Winter, 1986), pp. 76-77.

9   Roman Catholic theology on the ways Jesus is present is expressed in the Constitution on the Sacred Liturgy of Vatican II, par. 7. *The Documents of Vatican II,* edited by Walter M. Abbott, S.J. (New York: America Press, 1966), p. 141.

CHAPTER TWO. GANDHI AND THE GOSPEL

Page
10   The epigraph at the beginning of the chapter is taken from Martin Luther King's "Pilgrimage to Nonviolence," contained in his book *Strength to Love* (Philadelphia: First Fortress Press edition, 1981), p. 150.

10   Gandhi's description of Christian missionaries is contained in *An Autobiography: The Story of My Experiments with Truth*, by Mohandas K. Gandhi (Boston: Beacon paperback edition, 1957), pp. 33-34.

11   Gandhi's contemporaries' description of Christian practices is taken from the article "Spiritualizing the Political: Christ and Christianity in Gandhi's *Satyagraha*," by Richard L. Johnson and Eric Ledbetter, in *Peace and Change*, Vol. 22, No. 1, January, 1997, p. 34.

11   Gandhi's recollections from his conversations in England are found on p. 68 of his *Autobiography*, cited earlier (in connection with p. 10).

11   Gandhi's interpretation of how he was a Christian is found in Louis Fischer, *The Life of Mahatma Gandhi* (New York: Collier Books, 1950), pp. 335 and 336.

12   Gandhi's description of his conversation with his son is found in *Non-Violent Resistance*, by M.K. Gandhi (New York: Schocken Books, 1951), p. 132.

13-14   Gandhi's explanation of *ahimsa* is taken from "Gandhi on Ahimsa," in Vol III, No. 2 (Summer, 1966) of *Truthseeker*, the newsletter of the M.K. Gandhi Institute for Nonviolence in Memphis, Tennessee. His grandson, Arun Gandhi, is Founding Director of the Institute and Editor of its newsletter.

14   Gandhi's observation about a person devoted to service is found on p. 48 of *Non-Violent Resistance* cited earlier (in connection with p. 12).

15   Gandhi's statement on Jesus' suffering is quoted in James W. Douglass, *The Nonviolent Cross: A Theology of Revolution and Peace* (New York, Macmillan, 1966), p. 55.

15   Louis Fischer's quote is from p. 279 of his *The Life of Mahatma Gandhi* cited earlier (in connection with p. 11).

15   The Douglass quote is from James W. Douglass, *The Nonviolent Coming of God* (Maryknoll, NY: Orbis Books, 1991), p. 16.

16   King on Gandhi is on p. 150 of his "Pilgrimage to Nonviolence" in *Strength to Love* cited earlier (in connection with p. 10).

CHAPTER THREE. AN EPIC CHANGE

18   The epigraph at the beginning of the chapter is from Mairead Corrigan Maguire, "Politics With Principles?" in *World Without Violence: Can Gandhi's Vision Become Reality?* edited by Gandhi's grandson, Arun Gandhi (Memphis, Tennessee: the M.K. Gandhi Institute for Nonviolence, 1994), p. 53.

21   The Nuclear Threat: "It is a dangerous illusion to think that the threat posed by nuclear weapons disappeared along with the Cold War... If the START II Treaty is ratified...there will still be roughly 20,000

Page

nuclear weapons in the world with an explosive yield of 400,000 Hiroshima-sized bombs by the year 2003. The roughly 8,500 strategic and tactical nuclear weapons to be maintained by the United States will, in the words of Secretary of State Warren Christopher, have 'a capacity to destroy civilization as we know it several times over.'" From *The Defense Monitor*, a publication of the Center for Defense Information in Washington, D.C., Vol XXIV, No. 8, Sept.-Oct. 1995, p. 1.

22   The term "culture of violence" was used in the Nov. 29, 1994 Pastoral Message of the U.S. Catholic Bishops, *Confronting a Culture of Violence: A Catholic Framework for Action* (Washington, D.C.: U.S. Catholic Conference, 1994).

24   Richard Deats, "The Global Spread of Nonviolence," in *Fellowship* (Journal of the Fellowship of Reconciliation), July/August 1996, p. 5. The whole article (pp. 5-12) is an excellent summary of twentieth-century nonviolence in the Philippines, Chile, Haiti, China, Burma, Israel/Palestine, South Africa, and Eastern Europe.

CHAPTER FOUR. THE CHALLENGING SELF

25   The epigraph at the beginning of the chapter is from Helen Caldicott, *Missile Envy: The Arms Race and Nuclear War* (New York: Bantam Books edition, 1986), pp. 250-251.

25-26   The references to Satan by André Gide and René Girard are from Gil Bailie, *Violence Unveiled: Humanity at the Crossroads* (New York: Crossroad, 1995), p. 204.

26   Richard Woods, O.P., *The Occult Revolution: A Christian Meditation* (New York: Herder and Herder, 1971), p. 143.

26   Israel W. Charney, *How Can We Commit the Unthinkable? Genocide: the Human Cancer* (Boulder, CO: Westview Press, 1982), p. 26.

27-29   Thomas Aquinas analyzes the Capital Sins in his *Summa Theologica*, Part I-II, ques. 84, art. 5.

28   Gandhi's quote is on p. 46 of his *Non-Violent Resistance* cited earlier (in connection with Chapter Two, p.12).

29   Dorothy Day's observation is taken from *A Penny a Copy: Readings from the Catholic Worker*, edited by Thomas C. Cornell, Robert Ellsberg, and Jim Forest (Maryknoll, NY: Orbis Books, revised and expanded edition, 1995), p. 281.

31   Edward Schillebeeckx, O.P., a renowned Dutch theologian and one of the architects of Vatican II renewal, made this remark at an international conference on Peace Spirituality at Nassogne, Belgium, in 1984. He said that the peace of Christ, in our time, consists "in an inward discontent, in a prophetical protest against the situation as it is, and which is precisely not right the way it is." Edward Schillebeeckx, O.P., "In Search of the Salvific Value of a Political Praxis of Peace," in *Peace Spirituality for Peacemakers* (Antwerp, Belgium: Omega Press, 1985), p. 25.

CHAPTER FIVE. NO GOOD VIOLENCE

Page

32   The epigraph at the beginning of the chapter by Jeannette Rankin, the only member of Congress to vote against U.S. entrance into both World Wars, is from *Seeds of Peace: A Catalogue of Quotations*, compiled by Jeanne Larson and Madge Micheels-Cyrus (Philadelphia: New Society Publishers, 1986), p. 5.

33   For Walter Wink's description of the myth of violence as redemptive, see his *Engaging the Powers* (Minneapolis: Fortress Press, 1992), pp. 13-31.

33   Joseph Campbell has written about what he called the War Myth and the Peace Myth, in "Mythologies of War and Peace," *Myths to Live By* (New York: Bantam Books, 1972), pp. 174-206.

33   Senator Phil Gramm made this remark in his speech to the 1992 Republican National Convention, quoted in Ched Myers, *Who Will Roll Away the Stone? Discipleship Queries for First World Christians* (Maryknoll, NY: Orbis Books, 1994), p. 9.

34   Retired Memphis police lieutenant Jim Anderson's remark was quoted in the article "Gun class aims for smarts, not shots" in the Memphis *Commercial Appeal*, Dec. 9, 1996, p. A1.

34   Daniel Berrigan, *The Dark Night of Resistance* (Garden City, NY: Doubleday, 1971), p. 77.

34   See Harrison Salisbury's description of the luxurious life of Mao Zedung in his book *The New Emperors: China in the Era of Mao and Deng* (Boston: Little, Brown, 1992), especially Part Two: "The Secret Life of Zhongnanhai."

35   Gil Bailie, winner of the 1996 Pax Christi Book Award for *Violence Unveiled*, made this remark in an interview with the author in the *Catholic Peace Voice*, quarterly publication of Pax Christi-USA, Fall, 1996, p. 8.

35   Daniel Berrigan, "From a Korean Prison," talk given at Cornell University, May, 1976, cited in Ronald Peter Gathje, *The Cost of Virtue: The Theological Ethics of Daniel and Philip Berrigan* (Ann Arbor, MI: UMI Dissertation Services, 1994), p. 271.

36   Gil Bailie's quote is from p. 8 of the same interview in the *Catholic Peace Voice* cited above (in connection with p. 35).

36   Gandhi, from p. 39 of the article in *Peace and Change* cited earlier (in connection with Chapter Two, p. 11).

37   Daniel Berrigan, "Who Dies First: the Gunman or the Victim?" in *The Center Magazine*, Vol. 19, May-June, 1986, p. 22.

37   Gil Bailie from p. 9 of the same *Catholic Peace Voice* interview cited earlier (in connection with p. 35).

38   The continuum of "warism" to "pacifism" is described by Hamline University professor Duane L. Cady in *From Warism to Pacifism: A Moral Continuum* (Philadelphia: Temple University Press, 1989).

38   Joan Baez, "Three Cheers for Grandma!" in *What Would You Do?* by John H. Yoder and others (Scottsdale, PA: Herald Press, 1983), p. 62.

CHAPTER SIX. THE CITY OF GOD REVISITED
Page
41   The epigraph at the beginning of the chapter is from the words of
         Sam Keen in his book *Hymns to An Unknown God: Awakening the
         Spirit in Everyday Life* (New York: Bantam Books, 1994), p. 236.
41   The source of *City of God (De Civitate Dei)* quotes in this chapter is
         The City of God by St. Augustine (Garden City, NY: Image Books edi-
         tion, 1958).
41   City of the Flesh, City of the Spirit: *Ibid.*, Book XIV, Chap. 1 (p. 295).
42   Two societies produced by two loves: *Ibid.*, Book XIV, Chap. 28 (p.
         321).
42   Characteristics of both cities: *Ibid.*
43-44   Rosemary Ruether's observation is referred to in Mary Hembrow
         Snyder, *The Christology of Rosemary Radford Ruether* (Mystic, CT:
         Twenty-Third Publications, 1988), p. 68.
44   Sam Keen describes the Compassionate Commonwealth on pp. 235-
         245 of his *Hymns To An Unknown God* cited above (in connection
         with the epigraph at the beginning of this chapter).
45-47   The analysis of Jesus' teaching about turning the other cheek, handing
         over your cloak, and going the second mile was first called to my atten-
         tion in Walter Wink's *Violence and Nonviolence in South Africa: Jesus'
         Third Way* (Philadelphia: New Society Publishers, 1987), Chap. 2.

PART TWO: PERSONAL NONVIOLENCE
49   The epigraph at the beginning of Part Two is from the German
         Redemptorist priest Bernard Häring, a leading Catholic moral the-
         ologian after Vatican II, in his book *The Healing Power of Nonviolence*
         (New York/Mahwah: Paulist Press, 1986), p. 70.

CHAPTER SEVEN. CLOSING DOORS SOFTLY
50   The epigraph at the beginning of the chapter is from *The Gospel and
         the Struggle for Peace: Training Seminar in Evangelical Non-Violence
         and Methods of Engaging in It*, by Jean and Hildegarde Goss-Mayr,
         published by the International Fellowship of Reconciliation, 1990, p.
         33.
50   The quote from Lao Tzu is Huston Smith's version of the first lines of
         Chapter 27 of the *Tao Te Ching* cited above (in connection with
         Chapter One, p. 6): "A good runner leaves no tracks. A good speech
         has no flaws to censure." Huston Smith, using another translation,
         gives the quoted version in his book *The World's Religions* (New York:
         Harper San Francisco, 1991), p. 209.
53   Sr. Mary Lou Kownacki, O.S.B., Director of the Alliance of
         International Monasticism and former National Coordinator of Pax
         Christi-USA, used this image in a retreat she led for the Memphis
         chapter of Pax Christi in 1988.
54   Ellen Goodman wrote about the vow of civility in her syndicated col-
         umn which appeared as "Comeback of Civility?" in the Memphis
         Commercial Appeal, Jan. 3, 1997, p. A6.

Page

55-56   Gandhi's words on eating are quoted in *Truthseeker,* Vol. II, No. 3, p. 2, cited earlier (in connection with Chapter Two, p. 13-14).

56   Alan Watts, *Does It Matter?* (New York: Random House, Vintage Books edition, 1971), p. 28.

CHAPTER EIGHT. "DIFFICULT" PEOPLE

58   The epigraph at the beginning of the chapter is found on p. 181 of *A Penny A Copy,* cited earlier (in connection with Chapter Four, p. 29).

58   Mahadev Desai's reflection is from Judith M. Brown, *Gandhi: Prisoner of Hope* (New Haven and London: Yale University Press, 1989), p. 286.

62   Sam Keen's observation is from p. 114 of his *Hymns To An Unknown God* cited earlier (in connection with Chapter Six, p. 41).

CHAPTER NINE. NEGOTIATION NOW

66   Dorothy Day's remark is from p. 181 of *A Penny A Copy,* cited earlier (in connection with Chapter Four, p. 29).

66   The quote from psychiatrist Arthur Kornhaber is contained in an interview with him published in *Modern Maturity,* Jan.-Feb., 1997, p. 56.

66   The Martin Luther King quote is on p. 69 of *A Testament of Hope,* cited earlier (in connection with Chapter One, p. 7).

67   Dorothy Day spoke of enduring the "penance" of the pinpricks of community living. See the epigraph at the beginning of Chapter Eight.

67   Roger Fisher and William Ury, *Getting to Yes: Negotiating Agreement Without Giving In* (New York: Penguin Books, 1983), p. xi.

68   *Ibid.,* pp. 6-7.

71   Martin Luther King often spoke of creative tension, e.g., in his "Letter from Birmingham City Jail," on p. 291 of *A Testament of Hope,* cited earlier (in connection with Chapter One, p. 7).

CHAPTER TEN. SURVIVING OUR ENEMIES

74   The epigraph at the beginning of the chapter is from p. 65 of Thomas Merton, *Gandhi on Non-Violence* cited earlier (for the epigraph at the beginning of Part One).

76   The Center for Defense Information quote is from p. 3 of *The Defense Monitor,* Vol. xxiv, No. 1 cited earlier (in connection with Chapter Three, p. 21).

79   Angie O'Gorman described her experience with a would-be attacker in the video "Nonviolent Response to Personal Assault," produced by Pax Christi-USA in 1987.

79   Richard B. Gregg, *The Power of Nonviolence* (London: James Clarke and Co., second revised edition, 1960), p. 44.

CHAPTER ELEVEN. PRO LIFE—ALL LIFE

Page

82   The epigraph at the beginning of the chapter is from Shelley Douglass, "A World Where Abortion Is Unthinkable," in *Nonviolence in America: A Documentary History*, revised edition, edited by Staughton Lynd and Alice Lynd (Maryknoll, NY: Orbis Books, 1995), p. 339.

83   Gordon C. Zahn's articulation of a consistent life ethic, a pro-life stance across the board, is found in the essay "A Religious Pacifist Looks At Abortion," in his book *Vocation of Peace* (Baltimore: Fortkamp, 1992). The quotes here and on the next page are found on pages 68 and 77. Gordon Zahn, Professor Emeritus at the University of Massachusetts-Boston, was one of the few Catholic conscientious objectors during World War II. He was a co-founder, with Eileen Egan, of Pax Christi-USA.

84   Sally Miller Gearhart, "The Future—If There Is One—Is Female," in *Reweaving the Web of Life: Feminism and Nonviolence*, edited by Pam McAllister (Philadelphia: New Society Publishers, 1982), pp. 276-7.

85   Leah Fritz, "Abortion: A Woman's Right to Live," *ibid.*, p. 395.

86   The quote from Shelley Douglass is found on pp. 339-40 and 343 of her essay cited above as the epigraph at the beginning of this chapter.

87   The bishops' statement is found on pp. 5-6 of *Confronting a Culture of Violence*, cited earlier (in connection with Chapter Three, p. 22).

88   The one-page Pax Christi-USA Statement on Abortion was issued by the National Council of Pax Christi-USA at their August 11, 1989 meeting, held in conjunction with the National Assembly at Seattle University in Seattle, Washington. It is available from the Pax Christi National Office (532 W. 8th St., Erie, PA 16502).

CHAPTER TWELVE. NONVIOLENT CONFRONTATION

90   The epigraph at the beginning of the chapter is from Daniel Berrigan, "The Vocation of the Servant: Isaiah's Call to the Nations," in *Sojourners*, Jan. 1989, p. 18.

90   Publication information on the bishops' Pastoral Message is given earlier, in connection with Chapter Three, p. 22.

92   *Ibid.*, p. 15.

94   The Ched Myers quote is from p. 247 of his *Who Will Roll Away the Stone?* cited earlier (in connection with Chapter Five, p. 33).

95   Gandhi wrote: "Nonviolence is the law of our species as violence is the law of the brute," on p. 133 of *Non-Violent Resistance* cited earlier (in connection with Chapter Two, p. 12).

95   Carroll Dozier, the first bishop of the Catholic diocese of Memphis, said he wanted the new diocese to be built solidly on the pillars of peace and justice. He issued his first pastoral letter, on peace, just before Christmas of 1971, his first year as bishop. In it he wrote, "We must squarely face the fact that war is no longer tolerable for a Christian." The title of this pastoral letter, "Peace: Gift and Task,"

Page

foreshadowed the 1983 pastoral of the U.S. Catholic Bishops: "The Challenge of Peace: God's Promise and Our Response." Bishop Dozier's pastoral letter can be obtained from the Diocese of Memphis (P.O. Box 341669, Memphis, TN 38184-1669).

PART THREE: OUR BEST INTEREST

99   The epigraph at the beginning of Part Three is taken from p. 56 of Martin Luther King's *Strength to Love*, cited earlier (in connection with Chapter Two, p. 10).

CHAPTER THIRTEEN.   NONVIOLENT MONEY

100   The epigraph at the beginning of the chapter is taken from *Treasury of Religious Quotations*, compiled and edited by Gerald Tomlinson (Englewood Cliffs, NJ: Prentice Hall, 1991), p. 161.

103   The quote from Lao Tzu is from ch. 9 of the *Tao Te Ching*, p. 61 in the edition cited earlier (in connection with Chapter One, p. 6).

103   The quotes from Gandhi are taken from p. 46 of his *Non-Violent Resistance* cited earlier (in connection with Chapter Two, p. 12).

103   The Vatican II document referred to is *Gaudium et Spes*, the Pastoral Constitution on the Church in the Modern World, para. 26, found on p. 225 of the *Documents of Vatican II* cited earlier (in connection with Chapter One, p. 9).

105   Eileen Egan, "Property and Poverty," on p. 246 of *A Penny A Copy* cited earlier (Chapter Four, p. 29). Eileen Egan worked for many years with Catholic Relief Services. She was a personal friend and associate of Dorothy Day, and co-founder with Gordon Zahn of Pax Christi-USA.

106   King's disposition of his $54,600 Nobel Peace Prize money was to SCLC, SCNN, CORE, the NAACP, the National Council of Negro Women, and the American Foundation for Peace. Cf. Stephen B. Oates, *Let the Trumpet Sound: The Life of Martin Luther King, Jr.* (New York: New American Library, 1982), p. 312.

CHAPTER FOURTEEN.   NONVIOLENT TIME

107   The epigraph at the beginning of the chapter is from p. 218 of *Seeds of Peace*, cited earlier (in connection with Chapter Five, p. 32).

110   Stephen Covey, author of *The Seven Habits of Highly Effective People*, suggested the compass rather than the clock image in *First Things First: To Live, To Love, To Learn, To Leave a Legacy*, by Covey et al. (New York: Simon and Schuster, 1994), p. 16.

112   Tony and Robbie Fanning, *Get It All Done And Still Be Human: A Personal Time-Management Workshop* (Menlo Park, CA: Kali House, 1990), p. 56.

113   The Stephen Covey quote is from p. 35 of *First Things First* cited above (in connection with p. 110).

CHAPTER FIFTEEN. TELLING IT LIKE IT IS
Page
115   The epigraph at the beginning of the chapter is paraphrased from
       Book IV, Chap. 4 of *The City of God,* p. 88 in the edition cited earlier
       (in connection with Chapter Six, p. 41).
115   *Ibid.*
117   The Philippine church leaders' statement is contained in the
       International Solidarity News Digest published by the International
       Solidarity Network Desk of the Association of Major Religious
       Superiors of the Philippines (Quezon City, Philippines), November,
       1996, pp. 4-5.
118   The quote from Augustine is taken from Book XV, Chap. 4, on p. 327
       of the *City of God* edition earlier above (in connection with Chapter
       Six, p. 41).
118   The quote from the 1954 Doolittle Report to the Hoover Commission
       is found in Book I of *Foreign and Military Intelligence: Final Report of
       the Select Committee to Study Government Operations* (Washington,
       D.C.: Senate Report No. 94-755, 1976), p. 9.
119   Charney, p. 26 of *How Can We Commit the Unthinkable?* cited earlier
       (in connection with Chapter Four, p. 26).
119-120 John le Carré, *The Tailor of Panama* (New York: Alfred A. Knopf,
       1996), p. 71.
120-121 The Philip Berrigan quote is from his article "The Corporatization of
       the World" in *The New Year One,* publication of the Jonah House,
       Baltimore, MD, August, 1996, p. 4.
122   Daniel Berrigan, *Whereon to Stand: The Acts of the Apostles and
       Ourselves* (Baltimore: Fortkamp Publishing, 1991), p. 20.

CHAPTER SIXTEEN. POLITICAL AWARENESS
124   The epigraph at the beginning of the chapter is from p. 111 of *Seeds
       of Peace* cited earlier (in connection with Chapter Five, p. 32).
125   The quote from Gandhi is taken from p. 236 of Sam Keen, *Hymns to
       an Unknown God* cited earlier (in connection with Chapter Six, p.
       41).
126   Ruth Leger Sivard, *World Military and Social Expenditures 1996*
       (Washington, D.C., World Priorities), p. 39.
127   The Defense Monitor quote is from p. 2 of the Feb. 1996 issue of *The
       Defense Monitor* cited earlier (in connection with Chapter Three, p.
       21).
127   The military officer's quote is from *op. cit.,* April-May, 1996, p. 7.
128-129 Excerpts from Dean Alison Boden are from her sermon reprinted in
       Criterion (Journal of the University of Chicago Divinity School),
       Autumn, 1995, pp. 13-15.
129   Ched Myers, p. 276 of *Who Will Roll Away the Stone?* cited earlier (in
       connection with Chapter Five, p. 33).
129   The quote from Andrew Carnegie is taken from a PBS television pro-
       gram about him, "The Richest Man in the World," which aired on
       January 20, 1997, reported in the Memphis *Commercial Appeal:* "The

Page

Sinner/Saint" by Tom Walter, Jan. 20, 1997, p. C2.

130   Albert Nolan, O.P., who was elected Master General of the Dominican Order and resigned after one day to continue his work with the poor in South Africa, is quoted on p. 282 of Ched Myers, *Who Will Roll Away the Stone?* cited earlier (in connection with Chapter Five, p. 33).

131   "Catholic teaching has little to say to capitalism," *National Catholic Reporter*, Nov. 22, 1996, p. 24.

CHAPTER SEVENTEEN. TOGETHER WE CAN

134   "God loves our difference: we should too, rabbi says," excerpts from a sermon by Rabbi Micah Greenstein, printed in the Memphis *Commercial Appeal*, May 26, 1996, p. A11.

135   Matthew Fox, *Confessions: The Making of a Post-Denominational Priest* (New York: HarperSan Francisco, 1996), p. 47.

136-137 Roger Rosenblatt (Parsons Family University Professor at Southampton College of Long Island University), "The Admiration of Others," in *Modern Maturity*, January-February, 1997, p. 22.

137   Donald Cabana's conversion from state executioner to opponent of capital punishment is described in his book *Death at Midnight* (Boston: Northeastern University Press, 1996).

137   The quote from Ched Myers is on p. 170 of *Who Will Roll Away the Stone?* cited earlier (in connection with Chapter Five, p. 33).

137   Albert Camus, "Neither Victims Nor Executioners," which first appeared in the fall of 1946 in *Combat*, the daily newspaper of the French Resistance, was translated and reprinted in *Liberation*, an Independent Monthly, ©1960, p. 23.

138   Leonardo Boff, *Way of the Cross—Way of Justice* (Maryknoll, NY: Orbis Books, 1982), p. 16.

138   The quote from Gil Bailie is taken from p. 9 of his interview in the *Catholic Peace Voice* cited earlier (in connection with Chapter Five, p. 35).

CHAPTER EIGHTEEN. THE FUTURE IS NOW

140   The epigraph at the beginning of the chapter is from the song "The Impossible Dream" from the 1966 musical *Man of La Mancha*.

140   Deepak Chopra, *The Seven Spiritual Laws of Success: A Practical Guide to the Fulfillment of Your Dreams* (San Rafael, CA: New World Library, 1994), p. 61.

142   The quote from Martin Luther King is on p. 34 of his book *Strength to Love* cited earlier (in connection with Chapter Two, p. 10).

142   The Daniel Berrigan quote is on p. 251 of Ronald Peter Gathje, *The Cost of Virtue: The Theological Ethics of Daniel and Philip Berrigan* cited earlier (in connection with Chapter Five, p. 35).

143   The quotes from Michael Dowd are from his book *Earthspirit: A Handbook for Nurturing an Ecological Christianity* (Mystic, CT: Twenty-Third Publications, 1991), pp. 14-15.

144   *Ibid.*, p. 24.
144   The Gandhi quote is contained on p. 29 of James Douglass, *The Nonviolent Coming of God,* cited earlier (in connection with Chapter Two, p. 15).
145   The quote from Martin Luther King is on p. 35 of his book *Strength to Love* cited earlier (in connection with Chapter Two, p. 10).
145   The Douglass quote is from *ibid.,* p. 178.
145   The Charney quote is from p. 47 of his *How Can We Commit the Unthinkable?* cited earlier (in connection with Chapter Four, p. 26).

RECOMMENDED READING

Gil Bailie, *Violence Unveiled: Humanity at the Crossroads* (New York: Crossroad, 1995)

Daniel Berrigan, *Whereon to Stand: The Acts of the Apostles and Ourselves* (Baltimore: Fortkamp Publishing, 1991)

Judith M. Brown, *Gandhi: Prisoner of Hope* (New Haven and London: Yale University Press, 1989)

Thomas C. Cornell, Robert Ellsberg and Jim Forest, editors, *A Penny a Copy: Readings from the Catholic Worker* (Maryknoll, NY: Orbis Books, revised and expanded edition, 1995)

David Cortright, *Peace Works: The Citizen's Role in Ending the Cold War* (Boulder, CO: Westview Press, 1993)

James W. Douglass, *The Nonviolent Coming of God* (Maryknoll, NY: Orbis Books, 1991)

Michael Dowd, *Earthspirit: A Handbook for Nurturing an Ecological Christianity* (Mystic, CT: Twenty-Third Publications, 1991)

John Dear, S.J., *The God of Peace: Toward a Theology of Nonviolence* (Maryknoll, NY: Orbis Books, 1994)

Mohandas K. Gandhi, *An Autobiography: The Story of My Experiments with Truth* (Boston: Beacon paperback edition, 1957)

Sam Keen, *Hymns To An Unknown God: Awakening the Spirit in Everyday Life* (New York: Bantam Books, 1994)

Martin Luther King, Jr., *Strength to Love* (Philadelphia: First Fortress Press edition, 1981)

Staughton Lynd and Alice Lynd, editors, *Nonviolence in America: A Documentary History*, revised edition (Maryknoll, NY: Orbis Books, 1995)

Philip McManus and Gerald Schlabach, editors, *Relentless Persistence: Nonviolent Action in Latin America* (Philadelphia: New Society Publishers, 1991)

Ched Myers, *Who Will Roll Away the Stone? Discipleship Queries for First World Christians* (Maryknoll, NY: Orbis Books, 1994)

Gerard A. Vanderhaar, *Why Good People Do Bad Things* (Mystic, CT: Twenty-Third Publications, 1994)

James M. Washington, ed., *A Testament of Hope: the Essential Writings and Speeches of Martin Luther King, Jr.* (New York: Harper Collins paperback edition, 1986)

Walter Wink, *Engaging the Powers* (Minneapolis: Fortress Press, 1992)

Gordon C. Zahn, *Vocation of Peace* (Baltimore: Fortkamp, 1992)

INDEX

159

Of Related Interest. . .

Why Good People Do Bad Things
also by Gerard Vanderhaar

The author challenges readers to examine their lives and the effect of their actions (or in-action) on the social environment. Recommended highly by Bishop Walter Sullivan, this inspiring book will help all "good people" who read it understand the good/evil battle in their lives and help all to decide to act on behalf of justice in our world. Warning: book contains some shocking statistics.

ISBN: 0-89622-571-2, 160 pp, $9.95 (order B-73)

Healing Wounded Emotions
Overcoming Life's Hurts
Martin Padovani

The author, a priest-counselor, describes how our emotional and spiritual lives interact and challenges readers to live fuller, more satisfying lives. People involved in counseling will find this a valuable handbook, and individuals with psychological and religious conflicts will find guidance to resolve conflicts and foster peace.

ISBN: 0-89622-333-7, 128 pp, $7.95 (order W-22)
Audiobook: Three, 60-minute cassettes, 24.95 (order A-44)

Proclaiming Justice &Peace
Papal Documents from Rerum Novarum to Centesimus Annus
Edited by Michael Walsh and Brian Davies

The rich tradition of the church's social teaching over the last 100 years is recorded in this invaluable resource that encompasses 14 papal documents from Popes Leo XIII to John Paul II. These papal statements respond to a panorama of human needs, anxieties, and concerns.

ISBN: 0-89622-548-8, Paper, 522 pp, $19.95 (order C-98)

Available at religious bookstores or from:

 **TWENTY-THIRD PUBLICATIONS**
P.O. Box 180 • Mystic, CT 06355
1-800-321-0411
E-Mail:ttpubs@aol.com